My Escape to Love

Sylvia Duijm

My Escape to Love

Aspekt Publishers

My escape to Love

© Sylvia Duijm
© 2021 Uitgeverij ASPEKT / Aspekt Publishers
Amersfoortsestraat 27, 3769 AD Soesterberg, The Netherlands
info@uitgeverijaspekt.nl – http://www.uitgeverijaspekt.nl

Cover: Aspekt Graphics
Inside: Thomas Wunderink

ISBN: 9789464240856
NUR: 300

All rights reserved. No reproduction copy or transmission of this publication may be made without written permission.

To little Sylvia and Henkie

*For my two lovely daughters, who were
very much wanted*

And for Erik, the love of my life

Contents

Foreword *9*

Counting to ten *11*

Girlhood misery *41*

Denying my womanhood *75*

At the crossroads *101*

My relationships *119*

Free to love *171*

Afterword *187*

With thanks *193*

Foreword

Throughout my life, even in my mother's womb, I have known and felt that everything in life revolves around just one thing: Love. The love of others is the only thing that makes our short life bearable. I wanted to receive and give love, but that proved to be the most difficult thing of all! Not only for me, but for many others!

With that conviction, I decided to study orthopedagogy, a discipline practised in the Low Countries and amounting to a form of remedial education. I wanted to protect parents and children from suffering the pain that I experienced. I have developed my profession into the consolation and healing of people who have withdrawn into themselves (www.sylviaduijm.nl, www.sylviasonafhankelijkinstituut.nl). This book was primarily written for them, to show them they can find the road to freedom within themselves.

Baarn, Spring 2021
Sylvia Duijm

Counting to ten

It's full moon… Spring tide, January 1953. The water breaches the dykes. The North Sea flood. It was a major natural disaster. A lot of people died by drowning. At the same time, Ina Duijm-Graaf's waters broke and I was born at 7.10 am on 13 January in Westeinde Hospital, The Hague. I arrived in next to no time, speedy as ever since. I had a look suggesting "I'm here for the world and the world's here for me!" Brimming with confidence and eagerness!

Later my mother told me the nurse, the nun assisting the birth, had said "Watch out for that child, madam, she's going to be bossy." Those words heralded the great repression/suppression. Repression of my will, my vitality and the love that I felt and radiated. I was a lovely baby, tall with a mop of black curls, a heart-shaped mouth and inquisitive eyes. A pretty picture! A dangerous picture! In the end, I was to become a puppet, the motto being: "Everything we do is for your own good". The many house moves (by the time I was five, we'd already moved five times), time and again new surroundings, new school, new playmates, new rules, and to some extent my parents' unstable marriage, meant I lost my way and worse still, myself. My parents were not the great loves of each other's lives, but second choice. My father was in love with the mayor's daughter and my mother with the preacher. They maintained that their different backgrounds – father was from a middle-class family and mother from the Catholic upper-classes – were the reason why their dreams failed to materialise. My father explained that they had opted for each other "for fear of being left on the shelf". He met my mother when renting rooms in my grandmother's house. He was from Axel, a town in the southwest Netherlands, and was studying. My mother was attractive, a good match, and they liked each other. As confirmed by holiday snapshots depicting a 'radiant' couple. They were by no means soul mates, my father did whatever he wanted despite my mother's protests, and she followed. She did so throughout her life. I have an older sister, we're one-and-a-half years apart. My exact opposite. Shy, hesitant, a little fearful, highly introvert. We both felt like an only child. My sister mainly on a physical level – I was always outdoors playing somewhere, or else at boarding school.

I missed having a pal; they all knew what was good for me, she and my parents – I had three parents who didn't understand me and manipulated me, always 'for my own good'. What I wanted didn't count.

During the first six months of my life we lived in a park: Leeuwenberg park in The Hague. My father had borrowed money from my maternal grandmother's sister and had a detached house built, with a huge garden. Being a practical man, he kept a sheep to crop the grass. While we were living there my father got itchy feet: what with a small bourgeois family, his accountancy studies – he wanted to get out into the wide world, away from his responsibilities. He went to work for Shell, off to New Guinea. My mother sent him a weekly letter, a cheering letter… He was often despondent, sometimes he even wished he was dead.

Meanwhile the 'villa' had been sold and we were living with my grandma – my mother's mother. My mother was back to square one, with two small children. She didn't have a good time there, too claustrophobic. My grandmother, her sister Auntie Dien, mother's brother Jacques (who was to become my favourite uncle) and Fred (my favourite cousin). The house was very full, even though grandma had a stately residence with bells for the maid everywhere. Later I was to have a very good relationship with my grandmother, today she is one of my guiding lights.

We joined my father six months later. I was a year-and-a-half by then, still a pretty picture, with a will of my own. There is a photo of our arrival at Jefman airfield. We were walking down the steps, I in my mother's arms, my sister beside us and my father wearing a white, lightweight suit holding out his hands to take hold of me. He was over the moon to have his family complete again. His longing, plus his restlessness, proved very stressful and resulted in stomach trouble.

Our first house at Zeeweg was made from 'bila' (palm leaf) mats. Our second house, in the same street, was brick. I don't remember much, apart from the photos of myself, my friend Stef (the boy next door), my sister, our parents and their friends from the club.

The club, that was the place for my mother. There she would drink her gin and tonic, could be admired by other ex-pat men as an attractive woman…

There was one man, she called him 'Paay', for whom she felt more. She went no farther than being his sailing companion at regattas…I think. They won once, and my mother was awarded a silver compact plus mirror. I thought it was lovely. I wanted it to be mine later. At some stage the powder compact disappeared.

My father was away a lot, travelling, and my mother was happy out there. She disliked housework and there she had her staff. She also had an important 'job' – she was an announcer at Radio Sorong. It was the ex-pat channel representing their country of origin. She was able to make a 45rpm record, called a 'spoken letter', for her mother and family. My sister and I sang children's songs for it, like 'the ice cream man' song.

Sadly, my sister's ex-friend was supposed to convert the record onto a cassette, but the record disappeared: I never heard my 3-year old self singing 'the ice cream man' again. It was dismissed with 'pity', but never 'sorry'!

Back to the repression. Free spirit that I was, I didn't want to use a potty, to wee on command. I did do 'number 2' on the pot, I didn't want that in my knickers. I think I must have been around two years old. They took me to the local hospital, where I had to sit on the potty the whole day and was only allowed off when I had 'performed'. I wept and wept, and all I could see were my mother and sister peering at me through a small window. I couldn't understand why they didn't rush in and rescue me. I sat on the pot in a large room, weeping big tears, in the presence of a man in a white coat. I wasn't allowed home, I had to stay. I think they gave up after three days. I didn't want to be toilet-trained to order, at all costs!

My father was on leave and took our little family for a holiday in Australia – quite near to New Guinea. As free as a bird in the air... I wanted to use the toilet, my 'training' was complete. It was time, the time was ripe, I was ripe!

I don't remember much about the holiday in Australia. There are some photos of my mother in Capri pants, she always had a good figure and looked very feminine. My father also wore shorts but preferred to wear a tie as well. He wanted to demonstrate that he was not a labourer. When in Australia my sister developed a serious infection in her groin and the story goes that she needed an antibiotic injection every day. She also had a knee infection. There's a postcard of Sydney harbour as well. Part was fenced off, so we could swim, beyond that there were sharks. As a small child I found it very scary, but interesting too.

Back home to Zeeweg. Playing with my cat, Liplapje, my friend Stef. A small world, always filled with adventures. On one occasion we went exploring, farther than allowed. I stepped on a sharp rock (I called it the 'karang'), leaving behind a trail of blood. I still bear the scar and a swelling. I wasn't punished, they were glad I'd made it back home on my own. When I look at the photos of those days, I see a happy child. When on the ground, I always sat legs wide apart showing my white underpants. I loved my swing, my concertina, my bike, my cat and my friend Stef. I also liked cold chocolate milk and my 'moustache' betrayed if I'd been naughty – sneaked something out of the fridge.

I lived there until I was three or four years old. Returning to Holland for holidays, before the new, big move to Africa. We lived in an upstairs flat in Laan van Meerdervoort, in The Hague. My father had been posted to Persia, Iran as it is today, to Abadan. Uncle Pierre, my mother's brother, was there too.

Uncle Pierre's wife and children lived below us. He also worked for Shell. I missed my garden, my freedom, my parents' happiness at having their own space and pursuits. It was oppressive in The Hague. I couldn't breathe. I had to go to school, to kindergarten. My mother took me there, with my sister. It was horrible, the building, the strictness!

My mother was allowed to take me as far as 'the rope', beyond that was forbidden territory. The regime started beyond the rope. Walking in crocodile, forming lines in the classroom, doing what the teacher thought you should, you had to draw, thread beads, you were not allowed to do what you wanted. Strict, sitting up straight and only getting down when the teacher permitted. That was the start of a miserable time.

Every week a man turned up wearing a mask and carrying a bottle on his back. He came to work in the garden. I don't know exactly what happened, but I screamed blue murder. Wild horses couldn't get me to play in the garden on those days. My school break time was 'tailor-made' – shut in the classroom on my own.

When I look at photos from that period, I see myself on our balcony with a little watering can, the whole family lined up, no plants. And the 'acts' began, the start of 'compensation'. Screaming and protest proved worthwhile. If I had to go to the dentist, I either refused to open my mouth or else I bellowed. Mother panicked. What would the dentist think of her if she couldn't manage to get her child to open her mouth when ordered?! We'd return home, mission unaccomplished. My mother furious and in a tizzy. The story was recounted to my father that evening and punishment followed. I'm sure I was prepared to obey and be helpful, but the world was harsh, and others were not kind. Angry faces and imperious eyes – as a little four-year old, I didn't know how to deal with them.

I wasn't considered to be a good child, yet that is what I desperately wanted. Every bedtime I asked my mother, with a yearning look: "Mummy, am I a good girl?" I wanted a cuddle, a kiss, to be picked up and told "You're Mummy's good girl, sleep well and sweet dreams", or something like that.

My mother would just say "Yes and now go to sleep", without looking at me. And then she would walk away. For at least half an hour – while my family went crazy – I'd call "Mummy!" Always asking the same question. She could not reassure me. She didn't know how. I became quieter and quieter and withdrew into my own world. Still no-one thought I was nice and good. Today, working in remedial education, I know that a child without secure attachment bonds will begin by protesting, after which it despairs and then becomes indifferent. Fortunately, my character is such that I am willing to make the most of things and believe things can get better.

And they did! (It was a close shave. I was at the crossroads between life and death. Twenty-seven years old at the time).

Our departure was approaching. Shell sent my father to Africa, and we were leaving the upper floor apartment and going to live in Nigeria in a place called Umukurucha near Port Harcourt.

My father went out ahead to arrange housing. We had a nice brick bungalow there, L-shaped with French windows opening onto the enormous garden. We also had a garage with a car, a Ford Consul. My bike was also housed in the garage. In the garden there was a small brick house for our staff: the gardener, cook, assistant cook, cleaner. It means nothing when you're a child, that's just the way things are, neither good nor bad, normal! The left-hand part of the garden bordered a huge field. That field adjoined the 'blacks' village', as it was called. We lived in the white compound.

That field was in fact the reason for my first encounter with police and security. There was permanent policing. Black people were not allowed to cross the field to the white village. They had to make a whole detour, taking at least an extra hour. I never understood what was going on and when I sometimes saw people sneaking through our garden, I said nothing. I thought they were clever. Africa was less safe and relaxed than New Guinea. The police, the guards in the village, the segregation between black and white. I sensed it, as a five-, six-year old, the difference with New Guinea also affected my mother; here she was one of many women, she was no longer stood out, as she had when she was a broadcaster in Sorong. In those days my father used to film us, and you can see the tension in her appearance and behaviour. Now I could go my own way again, but differently. I encountered teasing for the first time. I went by bike on my own to the English school in the village. Probably a kilometre as the crow flies. There I went through part of kindergarten and the first form of elementary school. I had a pretty, kind teacher, Miss Visser. She taught kindergarten and first form in one. I always had her as my teacher there. I had a friend, Henk. I called him Henkie. We were inseparable – as I had been with Stef. We also went to the toilet together. It caused a great commotion and we were emphatically forbidden ever to do it again. We obeyed. But Henkie was easy to manipulate. I had a little cart and if he refused to pull it – and me – I'd say, "if you don't pull the cart I won't marry you". And he'd start pulling, though I never married him…

I enjoyed school, we began early and ended early. The return journey home was a problem and often very frightening. But more later. What I remember about school is that when the headmistress came into the classroom we had to stand and say: "Good morning, Miss MacFarling!" It all comes back to me. I had a friend called Anneke; we were as thick as thieves. Also, you played with the children of your parents' friends. The parents would eat together, or else there was a party, or something at the club. There would be an appropriate film and fun for the children, as well as for the parents. If we had guests, which was often, everyone ate and drank a lot. My mother would put a pair of scales in the sitting room and a very fat man was expected to keep on eating until he weighed 100 kilos! In fact, when travelling by helicopter, that man had to sit in the middle to keep the balance.

Going home after school. I can't recall the exact details, but the trip was always full of suspense. Two streets from ours there was a street with a ditch. Three boys would be waiting for me in the ditch, not always, but often. I sometimes managed to keep out of their firing line, my heart racing. Sometimes they'd grab me off my bike and the baiting began. I never cried, but I was very scared. I'd claim I had to do my homework, told them I'd never tell on them and at some stage it was over.

When children came to play there were often a lot of them and of all ages. One time someone told me to say to the cook "you're a black monkey", he'd like to hear that. So of course, I did. The police from the field were called in and after several hours things calmed down. My parents punished me severely.I can't remember what the punishment was, punishments were frequent.

We also celebrated 'Sinterklaas'(the traditional Dutch festivity in December when children who have behaved well throughout the year receive presents). In those days St. Nicholas was accompanied by 'Black Petes'. We didn't usually have them, but if we did, they weren't really black, but had black painted faces. The celebrations started with us putting out our shoes in the hope of receiving presents in them. In the Netherlands children place their shoes in front of the fireplace, but we didn't have one in Africa. Instead, there were French windows through which the Petes could enter. I did my very best for Sinterklaas. Putting water and a carrot out for his horse, writing a wish list and making a nice drawing. Exciting! Would I get something? We didn't have the same goodies as in Holland, but you did at least get a small gift in your shoe. My sister got presents, I generally got a letter. A letter saying, I hadn't been a good girl, that I should try harder and then there would be a present. It didn't seem fair. I didn't understand. It made no difference whether I did my best, my parents didn't notice. It was always my fault, whether I was to blame or not. The following year my sister told me Sinterklaas didn't exist. She couldn't bear for me to leave me in my own little world, too difficult for her.

Photos from that time show me as withdrawn from the family, or else the very opposite – holding my mother's arm or hand. I did so want to feel her love, so very much. I didn't really know what it was and sought it in vain.

The real Sinterklaas festivities were held every year in splendid fashion at the club. There I did get a present. The Queen's birthday was also celebrated in style. A mock-up of Amsterdam was built in cardboard. All the parents joined in. Someone, I don't know who, helped my mother to decorate our bikes with crepe paper in red, white and blue (our national colours), and we wore red-white-and-blue crepe paper skirts, topped by a white blouse and an orange kerchief. All kinds of activities were organised for young and old. I went fishing with a rod and magnet in a paddling pool, we had plank races, clambered through tyres – during which I tore my pretty skirt. I have happy memories of days like that. Between times we returned to Holland for around six weeks' holiday, living in temporary accommodation in The Hague.

I developed eczema behind my ears at that time, and often had tummy ache. I can picture myself standing at the bay window of that house. Dreaming, looking out, dreaming about "who thinks I'm a sweet girl?" Back to Africa. The eczema passed and so did the stomach ache, even though no-one thought me a sweet girl, as I dreamt they might. I did have enough space again and was able to relax. Every week my sister and I went to Brownies in our brown uniforms. We were also taken once a week in a VW van to catechism instruction from the nuns in the hills. My mother went with us. I don't recall much, though I can still recite Our Father and Hail Mary in English. I do recall having a day off school, to be a mannequin in a fashion show, which, as is usually the case, culminated in a beautiful wedding dress – and I was the bridesmaid. And so the ex-pat wives had their extravagances. I also remember hoping for new white shoes for the occasion. There was a hole in my sole and there wasn't a local cobbler. Pity, no new shoes. I can still picture it, hating as I did to walk on worn out shoes.

When I was little I was almost kidnapped by a black woman. She was carrying a basket of fruit on her head and I walked behind her, spellbound. That's what I remember. The story goes that she lured me and that acquaintances saw me walking out of the village with her. I suffered no adverse effects and clearly 'all's well that ends well'.

Uncle Pierre and his family didn't live far from us, in Owerri. We sometimes exchanged visits, and then stayed over. It was no great distance, but the roads were terrible. Dirt tracks and mud, and huge water buffalo wandered along the road.

My father worked precisely according to the rule book, no wonder he became an accountant! He did not have an easy time at Shell, as they used a different bookkeeping system. That was difficult for him, and so his contract was not renewed, and we returned to the Netherlands. Meanwhile civil war had broken out in the neighbouring country, Congo, and at a later stage also in Nigeria

– a conflict between Igbo and Hausa. We left at just the right time!

Back to the Netherlands, a country full of rules and little space. When I was small I didn't know my maternal grandmother – granny Graaf – very well. I'd hardly ever seen her. Back 'home', we went to live next door to her, in a house she owned. Grandmother owned a lot of houses, in my mind a whole street, and lots of parking garages and buildings! Grandfather, her husband, died young, of TB, and their children, seven in all except Koosje (later Jacques, the youngest) went to boarding school because of the disturbance they caused for ailing grandpa. That grandpa was said to have nose for business; he travelled abroad a lot and had a somewhat arrogant attitude. Photos depict him as a splendid grandpa! My mother always spoke of him with pride. However, her father's illness, her own character, boarding school and the pressure her own mother felt, meant that my mother never really came into her own. She was always anxious, solicitous with her tea and biscuits, and invisible too, as she put it "my contribution is behind the scenes". I never understood what she meant, though I do now, far better. She solved problems for my father – problems that sometimes arose from his impulsiveness. For instance, he bought a car. Not a sensible idea. My mother made sure the contract was cancelled.

When we were back in the Netherlands, I had to go to school. We lived in The Hague in a house next door to my grandmother. The chosen school, Maria School, was nearby. I went into the second form and my teacher was Miss Terstraat, the aunt of Pia, one of my friends.

Pia was nice, but the teacher… I never understood how she could possibly be related to Pia. Miss Terstraat was large, actually huge, broad, legs like tree trunks (with eczema), ugly teeth, grey hair and spectacles. In the classroom the desks were arranged in rows, they were dual desks seating two pupils each. The rows of desks, a big blackboard with Miss Terstraat beside it on a dais, made her look even bigger. A class of thirty, children from all backgrounds, united by faith. I was miserable from day one. The long days, staying at school during the lunch break – it was too far to walk home in between – the disgusting school milk, the discipline: it was a disaster. The teacher didn't take me seriously. I hadn't yet had my first Communion, I was behind in my Dutch and arithmetic, and sometimes spoke English. To start with the other children thought I was interesting, yet it was hard to make friends. Friendships had been forged in the first form and I was intruding. I always seemed to be intruding, between Marlene (father a pastry-cook) and Maaike (father a doctor)), they were friends and I trailed after them. I got on well with Pia, the teacher's niece. Almost all the children were from large Catholic families. Families like that were fun and busy, invariably with no room for me. Truusje, my friend who lived in the same street, was one of a family of twelve. There wasn't any room there for me either. Truusje often had to help out at home and if she was allowed to play it would be at my house if that was permitted. At home we always had to be quiet for my sister, who enjoyed studying and reading, and not playing. She never wanted to play with me! So, I was often expected to play outdoors, far from our front door.

My mother wasn't keen on my friends. I often went to the homes of children in big families, which my father also visited on behalf of the Society of St. Vincent de Paul, a voluntary organisation in the Catholic church. He was supposed to keep an eye on their parenting, money matters and whether support was needed from the church. I took those children home with me to play, giving them toys and invariably asking my mother "can … stay for dinner?" My mother didn't know how to act, and they didn't stay for dinner. She would get very angry with me and I didn't understand why. There was no communication. Everything was dismissed with "that's just the way it is" – one of my mother's sayings – or "because I say so and I'm the boss" – one of my father's sayings. In the second form, when Miss Terstraat was our teacher, something terrible happened. Once I pursued Anneke, a big girl from a big family, always smelly and with a runny nose. I hounded her, as if she were an animal, calling "snotty nose, snotty nose" in such a taunting way. I wasn't ever a real bully, I can't remember why I did it, but I do know I wouldn't ever tease someone for the sake of it, however easy it might have been. That's not in my nature. Anneke reported the incident to Miss Terstraat and she shouted at me, shook me and cursed me. She took a piece of chalk and wrote on the freshly-wiped right-hand blackboard words that took up the entire board: DUMB, with below that, SYLVIA DUYM. When people walked past our classroom they could read it. Groups of kids stood around laughing and pointing. I hadn't told anyone at home about it, I couldn't expect any support from them, and I was very ashamed. My sister told, I don't know why. For many years I didn't have much 'support' from her. She couldn't comfort me, hold my hand, make me feel that she, my big sister, would support her little sister. She was shy and anxious, and I was 'strange' – that was the excuse. My mother went to school and the horrible words were wiped off the blackboard. Not with a wet eraser. Miss Terstraat only did that when she wanted to write something important on the board, and so traces of the words were left. She was a spiteful person. I just managed to make it up to the next class. Into Miss Van Wijk's class. A nice teacher, who felt sorry for me, but didn't know how to give me a sense of security. She often called me 'the little lodger' because I was different. She liked me, she loved me as well. She wanted to make me happy. She sensed I was unhappy, possibly also sensing my longing for affection. I was restless, and she thought she could help me by thinking up all kinds of little chores. Instead of doing arithmetic I was allowed to water the plants, help the director delivering messages. And in the end, I stayed on another year with Miss Van Wijk, so I stayed down a class… My friends moved up and I was alone or intruding again. I had to start all over. I don't recall the second year in Miss Van Wijk's class too well. I made a friend, coincidentally her name was also Sylvia (father a pastry-cook). I liked going to her house and in the bakery, it was warm and smelled good, and we were allowed to taste things. Her father was a jovial, pleasant, plump man and was always so friendly, so cheerful! He was the first cheerful, friendly father I ever consciously experienced, and full of interest for Sylvia and Sylvia. At school the teacher no longer sent me off to do chores. At home things were not nice, not pleasant. It was dark, quiet and boring. I didn't like being at home. My mother was often tired, had a migraine, wanted peace and quiet. Every week a district nurse came to give her a liver injection. From the moment we arrived back in Holland, my father was out of work. He sent off a lot of applications and a dark mood hung over the house because of his lack of work. Maybe he received some kind of benefit, but my parents were inclined to be on edge if they had no control over a situation. Just imagine how on edge they were because of me! The greater the tension, the greater the solidarity. I do wonder sometimes if that was why I behaved the way I did. However, since father didn't have a job, mother decided we must live frugally. When I needed new shoes, we went to a certain kind of shop and the first thing she said when we entered was: "I'm looking for cheap shoes for my daughter".

Clearly that had an effect. I always go for what is expensive! My winter clothes were hand-me-downs from my cousin, Christa, and she was slimmer than me. Her winter coat in particular was too tight for me, but I had to wear it – and it earned me the nickname of 'chubby'. At home they thought it was normal and laughed about it. Not long ago I met up with Pitty. She used to be a childhood friend of my sister's, her only friend. She lives near my workplace, where I have worked as an untouchable. I had occasionally seen Pitty and in fact arranged to meet up with her when I heard her husband had died (though my sister had never again seen her since childhood). When Pitty saw the way I now look the first thing she said was: "they used to call you 'chubby'!" How children can suffer….

One day my mother, sister and I were visiting my father's parents – grandpa and grandma Duijm. Father wasn't with us. I never loved either of them. Grandma was penny-pinching and strict. When she took you to bed, you had to lie with your hands crossed, on top of the blanket. If they were under the bedclothes it wasn't decent, and God saw everything. Also, you wore pyjama bottoms reaching to your armpits, making it extremely difficult to play with your private parts – because that was of course what they were thinking of. You were served lemonade in the smallest glass and all she did was knit jumpers for Abbé Pierre "to achieve a high place in heaven". My grandfather was scared of his wife and therefore malicious with other people, and me in particular. He was impatient and short-tempered, as was my father even though he 'tried' to suppress it. I don't really don't know the real reason. I wasn't good, too noisy for granny and grandpa, and it was essential to know who was the boss. Grandpa would take me under his arm and carry me off screaming, while mother looked on and did nothing. In the garden there was a free-standing, dark shed where I was locked up. I was desperate, shrieked, hammered on the door to be let out. For years I didn't dare to use a loo with a locked door, scared that the door would stick, and I wouldn't be able to get out. I had nightmares for ages, waking screaming, panicking that I was 'locked away' and couldn't find the way out. Sometimes I even took a cupboard with me in my panicky flight. Those 'dreamt' panic attacks recurred regularly until well into my forties.

As I didn't have many friends and not much fun at home, I often went to visit Babs Vrolijk who lived across the road. She was married to Sander Vrolijk (the Dutch word 'vrolijk' means 'cheerful', but that name did not suit Sander at all). They had two young daughters, but I came for the mother. Babs and I had a mutual friend, the milkman. I had ballet lessons, but no-one in our house was interested in my dancing accomplishments. Only the milkman was. When I was home, around 4 pm, he would bring the milk into the kitchen. My mother usually bought unbottled milk, as it was cheaper. I don't know she then did, because she wasn't around. I'd take off my dress and stand there in my vest and petticoat. Put on Swan Lake and dance for the milkman. It was pure, so affectionate. He watched and admired me as if I were his daughter. I felt someone noticed me. Babs' husband was dull, the milkman was cheerful and caring.

Babs often stood in the doorway a good quarter of an hour, her arms crossed, talking to him, laughing, being happy. Neighbourhood gossip and insinuations at home were unambiguous. "The milkman brought more than just milk, for sure!" I was allowed to eat at Babs' house one day, Sander had something office-related and would be coming home later. Other than that, there she sat with that man, wasting away, all year long. Babs loved me like a younger sister or girlfriend. I was eight or nine at the time, and she discussed her worries, sorrows, disappointments with me. I understood her, and I was her consolation. Babs taught me to sew on the sewing machine. Later I made quite a lot of clothes of the kind I didn't get from my parents: too modern, too sexy, and Babs helped me make them. Afterwards I went to visit the couple. Sander was still living there, but Babs had left him, flown the coop? I hope she found true love, knowing what a fine woman she was, a ray of sunshine who could have fun, but provide comfort too. Occasionally Sander can be found on the promenade at Scheveningen, singing gospel songs. He still looks lost and gloomy yet would seem to think he has found happiness.

As far as my sister was concerned, I felt the physical and emotional distance between the two of us and so wished it was different.I wanted a proper sister, I wanted to feel I had a sister. I wanted to cuddle up to her in bed, nice and cosy. But my sister did not set great store by things like that. If I really wanted, I was allowed in her bed, between the top sheet and her blanket, but not actually in the bed. She thought it was nasty. But she would join me in my bed, under the sheet instead of the prickly blanket – she didn't mind that. I think we may have joined each other in bed about four times, at my request. Between the bedrooms belonging to my sister and me there was a connecting door and she was the one who decided if it would be left open or not. Our parents regularly went out when we were in bed. I couldn't sleep until they were home again. When they were out I first checked if their pyjamas were still on their bed: I was always frightened of being abandoned, that they'd surreptitiously leave me behind. I was troublesome, and they didn't love me, but they did love my sister. They'd sneak in to collect her. All I could do was stay awake.

I played out my fears a couple of times a week with my dolls. If there was no-one for me to play with, I could play at home, but not disturb my sister. In the garden we had a worn canopy, brownish-yellow. It had belonged to my grandmother. I pretended that it was the canopy of my covered wagon. I sat there with my dolls. I was seven or eight years old at the time. I looked after my dolls well, we loved one another, and I always spoke to them encouragingly. I'd say: "I'll always take good care of you, you're safe with me, we must leave now, are you ready for the journey?", then the canopy would go up and we'd leave for the 'safe country'. At home they thought I was odd, with my games…

At night, as I fell asleep, I'd often hear a buzzzzzzing sound, and on the wallpaper above the mirror lots of little men with fiery eyes would appear, dancing crazily. I was scared, scared stiff, and begged them to go away. It didn't help, the buzzzzzzzing grew louder and the only solution was to crawl under my bed, then I didn't see or hear them. I didn't dare tell anyone, not even my grandmother, my favourite grandmother.

Grandmother – my mother's mother, granny Graaf – often took us to bed when my parents were out playing tennis or visiting friends. After all, she lived next door. Granny was small, had a large bosom, grey hair in a bun, a small mouth always pursed in a determined expression. Granny knew what she wanted, and she loved me. I sensed it. Granny understood me and often disagreed with my parents. She didn't say so, but I could tell from the way she looked. I can picture her, with a look that said, "how can you do that", but, just like my mother, she didn't put it into words. Her role was different, and times were different then too. I don't blame her. Granny helps me now. She is my guide in everyday things.

It was lovely when granny tucked me into bed. First, we'd have dinner with her and uncle Jacques, my mother's youngest brother. Then uncle Jacques would read to me from a book about the adventures of a cabin boy aboard a ship. Oh, so exciting and cosy, cuddling up to my uncle, who loved his little niece, as he liked to tell me and show me. Later I was to be the bridesmaid at his wedding! When grandmother tucked me up and gave me a loving kiss, she always said "sleep tight", and I felt very safe. As soon as she left, it was different, and I panicked, got out of bed to check that my parents' pyjamas were in place and stayed awake until they returned. For when there was a thunder storm, my grandma, knowing how scared I was, gave me a whistle. I could blow it at the first clap of thunder or flash of lightning. She said she heard me and came straight away. I believed my grandmother, she would never promise to do something and then not do so. One time she didn't hear my whistle, but she knew her little girl and came anyway!

My sister thought a lot of what I did was childish or nonsense and kept silent. She rarely took my side. That may well have been difficult at our age and in our family. We were allies on one occasion. By then grandma had died. It was boring at home. When I went to school, to that nice Miss Van Wijk, we passed by a convalescent home, 'het Sunneke', in our street. 'We' being Pitty, who lived near us, my sister Marjan and me. Pitty collected us and the three of us walked along together. I always waited at uncle Cor's window, pressed my nose against the window and called out "hello, uncle Cor" and waved. And he would wave back weakly. Uncle Cor wasn't a real uncle, but an unknown man who was a patient at the convalescent home. I saw him lying there and at some stage started waving and smiling at him. It turned out to be something special for him, our daily greeting. One day a nurse came out to say that the sick man would like to greet me in real life. I went in, his name was Cor and that's why we called him uncle Cor. He said he was so happy when I passed by twice a day and waved to him. Someone else who liked me and was pleased with me.

One day the bed was empty and uncle Cor was dead. I was very sad. My uncle Cor dead. The route to school was a sad one until I discovered the knocker on the door of a pub, Café Joris in the square, Koningsplein. But that was quite a different story: the pub owner was not at all pleased with me, he was furious when I banged the knocker yet again. What fun! Pitty and my sister also thought it was exciting.

By then my father had found a job in Rotterdam, at the Tax Office. It was in a street popularly termed Plukmekaalstraat, translating as Fleece-me street. How appropriate! My father was an assistant accountant. In the evenings he studied to become a registered accountant. Things didn't improve. Now I had to be quiet for my father, as was already necessary on account of my sister. My father studied in the attic, next to the little room where I liked to play during the day. The attic was above my sister's bedroom. If I was very quiet I was allowed to play there, at 'shop' with real products. I had a mini-shop, preferably selling shoes. But I had a problem: there were rarely customers because no-one at home wanted to play with me. Later on, not even parlour games. My father studied in the little room above my bedroom. Both rooms were small and mine was the coldest in the house. It faced north, was above the hall, and there was no heating.

My sister did have a heater because she studied and that meant she was cold. My father also had one. In addition, he paced up and down, not because it was cold but in order to assimilate his study material. I also pace up and down when I want to absorb something serious – and I teach other people to do so too.

I called my father's little study the 'peekaboo room' because there was a little heart-shaped opening in the door through which you could peek and quickly duck away your head. At the office my father had his own secretary. He was always talking about her, about how pretty she was, how good she was at her work. He referred to her at home as my 'little doll'. My mother said nothing. Once, on a Saturday evening, Dolly and her husband were visiting, they sat in the sitting room. They and my parents acted as if they were good friends. She had short curly blond hair, just like my mother, wore stiletto-heeled shoes, just like my mother, and did nothing but laugh, in a silly way. Not like my mother. She was the beginning of my father's sweethearts who visited under the guise of friendship. As a child I was aware of what was going on. When my cousins Katja and Christa came to stay (they'd lived with us in Africa) they slept in an extra foldaway bed in my sister's room. The door between our bedrooms would be open and we'd lie there chatting. I always recited 'erotic poetry', as I called it, often at the cousins' request. I'd start with Leo, my father's name, and Dolly, sharing the double sleeping-suit folly. What were they doing? Not just looking at each other – and we'd shriek with laughter. With me in my element. And then, inevitably, my father would come upstairs, hopping mad.

Or else my parents were already in bed next door to my sister's room where there were sliding doors – adjoining bedrooms. I would be dragged out of bed and banned to the attic to cool down. I didn't mind. I'd had such fun, it was worth it all. Perhaps that was the beginning of my willingness to pay the price for my private jokes – and perhaps other people's discomfort knowing I was right!

The year in Miss Van Wijk's class was over and I went up to the fourth form, conditionally, having stayed down a class. Miss Hassing – a second Miss Terstraat – was now my teacher. She was smaller, had even worse teeth and spat when she spoke. It was hell with Miss Hassing. Fortunately, a new girl came into our class – Monique. She was tall, very well developed, wore glasses that are still fashionable today (a kind of Ray Ban) and had an air of owning the entire world. That was what I wanted, and we became friends. Her parents were actors with the Haagse Comedie theatre company. They were divorced. Monique's mother always seemed to be relaxing on a chaise longue. We were allowed to make a noise, she just lay there, depressed. Monique taught me to do the twist. She thought I should be able to do it, it was part of our friendship. She lent me a single to take home to practise with. I have to grin about it now. Twisting at our house! I took her order seriously but wasn't taken seriously at home. The priest soon heard about my lapse, and though friendship with Monique wasn't exactly forbidden (my parents were too wise for that), there was a different solution. Problems at school increased. My confrontational behaviour – I was starting to understand adults and their power games better – became more frequent and stormy. Later my students,

Amsterdam dropouts, would have said "you didn't give a shit for anything or anyone!" The gym teacher in the fourth form was another unpleasant person. Her name was Miss Bots. Together with Monique I was one of the tallest in the class and we always stood at the back, horsing around. Miss Bots, like Miss Hassing, spoke 'with her mouth full of spray', as we called it. I found it so disgusting that one day I took an ice-cream umbrella with me for protection. Again, I was picked out of the row and, surprise, surprise, she started spitting as she fulminated. I took my little umbrella out of my cardigan and opened it saying, "Miss Bots *lost the lolly plot??*" while holding the umbrella in front of my face. I was dismissed into the corridor and off to the head teacher. My mother was summoned. We'd had our reports and I had a 6+ for conduct, and in the margin beside 'application': "Sylvia is making more of an effort". That afternoon we had handwork. All we did was make baby clothes, smocking. And this time we were knitting baby pants. I wanted to be a mother later, but then I'd buy ready-made pants! Not like the ugly ones I was making, full of holes because I dropped stitches – though I called the holes 'air-holes'. I had to undo the lot. I hated that nun. In order to punish her I proposed that everyone in the class should stamp on the wooden floor and drive her crazy. Everyone did indeed join in. And she went crazy. When asked whose idea it was I proudly put up my hand. I had to return my report and the 6+ for conduct was changed into a 4. My mother had to come to school yet again. She built up a 'close tie' with the headmaster, Mr. Walters. He was a small, nondescript little man with rabbit's teeth. He was cold, though claimed to love children. He tried to make a big, strong impression. But I'd sized him up. Once when he was frosty and unkind I called him a cold fish. And my mother was again invited to come to school. I wasn't scared any more. Indifference had set in. Of course, that phase also came to an end, but it took a while. The situation at home wasn't much better. I had a pair of penny shoes and I really liked wearing them. But because of my father's job, the quality of my shoes improved considerably. We then bought them at Guinee, a shoe shop for people with unusual feet and old unfashionable. Arch supports were added. I wasn't allowed to wear my old penny shoes, or only very occasionally. My father hid them, but I always managed to find them. When he came home from work in the evening I would be standing at the front door wearing my penny shoes and a look that said, "I'll jolly well do what I want". It wasn't at all pleasant at meal times either. My mother disliked cooking. It was always meat, potatoes and vegetables, and on Fridays fish or macaroni or potato salad. The latter was the worst. They always talked about share prices – that was the first thing my father checked when he came home. His work, my sister's successes at school, and then my mother would itemise all the day's dissatisfactions. Again, I'd be ticked off or punished for what had happened earlier in the day. My mother was the tattletale. There were often conflicts during the meal and it was always my fault. If I was given a hiding and said, "I didn't do it", my father would say no more. My sister sometimes said, "Sylvia didn't do it". But it made no difference. He was tired after his outburst of anger. Sometimes my father said: "If this goes on, I'll send you from the table!" And being a proud child, I'd say, "I'll go now" and pick up my plate. I don't recall what followed, probably too bad to remember.

My grandmother was sick by then; she wore a shawl. Granny had cancer of the throat and blue lines had been drawn on her neck where radiotherapy had to be directed. The shawl hid them. When granny tucked me up, I felt the shawl tickling me, but it didn't bother me – granny was there. I didn't realise how ill she was and she didn't show it. However, she did increasingly show her displeasure at the way I was treated. Every Wednesday afternoon I went, with a few neighbourhood children, to watch our favourite TV programmes at granny's house… and especially the programme presented by 'Auntie Hannie', who always waved to the audience when it was over – and we waved back! Then we were given cocoa and a boiled sweet. The sweets were made by the Kok company and the cocoa was served in tiny coffee cups. Granny was one of the few people in the street to have a television set. We also always celebrated the feast of St. Nicholas at her house, together with our favourite uncle Jacques. He had a girlfriend, her name was Trui (the Dutch word for 'jumper'). I was allowed to knit if I wanted, and I knitted a small jumper for him in blue wool. He thought it was wonderful. My cousin Fred was always there too. He made a lovely drawing in my autograph album. I was so proud and happy that someone had gone to so much trouble for me instead of just making some silly picture. At St. Nicholas, gifts are exchanged in the form of 'surprises' accompanied by a fitting poem. I remember getting one from my parents consisting of a toilet roll with a gift inside. My poem referred to the fact that I didn't take enough time to wipe my bottom properly – and the relevant consequences. Granny watched, embarrassed on my behalf. My comfort came from books about boarding schools of the Enid Blyton type – what fun the girls had! I requested, and received, such books. Which proved to presage my banishment.

The situation at school and at home was not good and I had to see the family doctor once a week: Dr. Twaalfsteen. I was almost 10 years old. My parents spilt the beans, as the saying goes. The implications were confusing – I understood what was said and yet I didn't. I didn't cotton on that I was being manipulated, it was all so cunning. I remember sitting with Dr. Twaalfsteen at school (would that not be considered 'strange' nowadays?), with my parents at his desk and then the 'consultation' began. Ending invariably with the announcement that I was to blame for my mother's migraines, to blame for my father's stomach trouble. And later I was to be to blame 'for their bad marriage'. The best solution would be boarding school. It was horrible at home. I felt very much alone, lonely, frightened. The books about boarding school, describing the fun the children had, seemed more appealing than staying at home and that nasty school. If I went up to the 5th form, there I'd be with Miss Steen and she was even worse than Miss Hassing. She was completely cold-hearted. My sister got on well with her. She got on well with everyone. She was quiet, withdrawn, unobtrusive. She did what she had to, never any more or any less. Then everything was always fine. She took no risks, fearful of rejection, disappointment. She was shy and scared. She didn't dare to phone friends or ask for anything from anyone. Perhaps, looking back, she was as lonely and anxious as I was, but just expressed it differently. Nor did she ask anything of our father and mother. They thought and acted on her behalf. She didn't have to do a thing. Not wash up, make her bed, set the table – nothing. When she got home from school, her room would be heated, her bike, later her moped, was brought in or taken out for her. Before bedtime my father walked round the block with her, so she would sleep well. My sister was termed 'invisible and ugly' and I was 'the stupid pretty one'. She got everything that was useful, attractive and appropriate for her age. Like a bike, a desk, roller skates, some moped, new clothes and so on. It had to be my birthday for me to get anything like that, or save up for it, and it didn't come from my parents. Aunt Mies, an old friend of my mother's (she was my godmother) gave me roller skates. And Uncle Pierre, my godfather, sometimes gave me a nice present. I recall a birthday gift from my parents: a bracelet that had cost one guilder and sixty cents. I'd seen it in the shop when we were buying a bag for my mother and I liked it. That's all I was worth! That's the picture, and a sad one for me.

They selected a boarding school. There weren't many combining a primary school that were reasonably affordable and not too far away. It was St. Joseph's school in Monster in South Holland province. Yet again tears streamed down my cheeks. It would be a black period in my life that damaged me until I was liberated.

Girlhood misery

I don't remember saying goodbye to the old school and my friends there. I assumed that when I was home at the weekends all would be well. Different. More fun, all welcome and me in particular! Well, it was indeed different. My fears grew, not only of being abandoned, but it was so unsafe there at the new school with the tyranny of the group. Keeping you in the dark about what a girl undergoes, physically and mentally, scaring you. You lose control of yourself and your surroundings, you learn – slowly – to deny yourself. Preparations for boarding school were interesting. I had to be measured for a uniform, a kind of KLM blue, a collarless jacket with a white blouse worn under it, a blue pleated skirt (too long). That was the outfit for Sundays and special school occasions. And then, three white pinafores, also for Sundays, and coloured ones for every day. I had no idea why I had to have a pinafore, my mother wore one when she cooked and I didn't have to cook. This time I got white lace-ups from Guinee, as well as a pair of smart brown shoes. The white ones were for Sundays. That too was new – we didn't have special Sunday clothes at home. And of course I had a small suitcase for when I was allowed home. I got the case I wanted, though normally I never got what I wanted. A matching satchel (a shoulder bag, as it's called nowadays) was also purchased. A beret was also part of the uniform, in red check. That might account for the fact that today I'm not keen on red checks. We also bought two white felt hats, one with a little band on the side and one with a feather. All this headgear including the beret was for wear to church. Apparently I had to go to church every other day. To early mass. Various aunts came to visit: three of my father's sisters, two of whom were nuns, and the eldest, aunt Julia, had entered a convent. In fact, 'behind bars', meaning she was shut away and not permitted into the 'normal' world. My paternal grandmother – the one who put us chastely to bed – was very proud of her daughters. Quite an achievement, having such brides of Christ!

The feeling of being shut away was something I had from the very first day at boarding school. At the time, we had a white Volkswagen, and I vaguely remember (the memory is so horrible that I've repressed it) being taken to school one Saturday afternoon by my parents and my sister. Wearing my beret and armed with my small case and satchel, with my father carrying my big brown case, which in the end remained there for six years. On arrival we were ushered into a parlour. A room containing a sideboard, a table with chairs round it, two armchairs and of course a large crucifix. It was horribly quiet, you could hear a clock ticking. The Sister Superior entered and greeted us. Rules were 'discussed': I would be allowed home for a weekend six weeks later, normally it was once a month, but not yet: I had to stay a bit longer "in order to settle in properly". I never settled in. I was allowed to receive mail and also to write home, time was specially set aside for letter-writing. Later it transpired that you received your letters opened, and letters for home had to be handed in, open (honesty was out of the question). Making and receiving phone calls was permitted in exceptional cases. My parents nodded knowingly and my father kept bowing to sister superior, I thought it was pathetic. We were given a conducted tour by a 'simple' nun. Various parents and children were walking round and it all felt like a dream, I couldn't grasp it all. There were two sections, one for the little children (primary school) and one for the big girls (MULO or middle school). I was allocated a cubicle which was for children of 8 to 9 years old. It had three partitions and a curtain. I think there were between 12 and 14 of such cubicles in that space. It had a bed and a shelf against the foot end of the bed, a chair and a washbasin with a mirror above. There was no room for a cupboard, that was in a different area. My parents and I unpacked my case and put my things in the cupboard – described as "having a nice time unpacking with your parents". As soon as the cupboard was arranged, that was that: to keep the farewells brief. You could accompany your parents/family as far as the front door, not alone but together with a nun, who held you tight so you couldn't fly away – and then I was truly alone… Indescribable: everything looked black and wet, nauseous, breathless, lifeless. Soon a bell rang and we were expected in the refectory, a dining room with tables and chairs for 8 people. There were about 60 girls present, ranging from 6 to 17 years of age. We were given lemonade made from concentrated syrup, and a Maria biscuit. I still hate those mean biscuits. More rules were explained to us, about table manners and the procedure at meal times. Every table had a 'table senior' appointed by Sister Maria, who was in charge of the refectory.

Sister Maria had various tasks. Also, she had a harelip and didn't much like children. She enjoyed scrubbing and calling the shots. Our recreation hours were also spent with her. After lemonade and biscuits we were introduced to our group. All of us between 6 and 12 or 13 were in one group. For recreation, as it was called, we were split into two groups. The very young ones, 6 to 10 years old, and the older girls who were in the higher classes. The first introduction involved the whole group. I am a kind person and I felt really sorry for the little ones. I suppressed my own distress. "My distress is nothing compared with theirs. So young and then away from home." They were the children of bargees and sometimes did not see their parents for very long periods. I comforted them. The rest of the day passed me by. In bed at night I cried myself to sleep, completely gutted. I wasn't yet frightened, just sad. "I want to go home." I wasn't the only one and that was some consolation. I heard more sobbing and tossing and turning. I went through the following days as if I were stunned, everything was different and strange, the names, the rooms, the children, the new school, life according to rules. Everything was planned down to the last minute and I was used to following my impulses. Spontaneously. I was a spontaneous child that had to become a puppet, in order that she could be manipulated into saying and doing what adults wanted… just that. Just dead.

At my new school[1*], the School of the Sacred Heart, I was in Sister Gisela's class. An indeterminate person.

1* Translator's note: not all boarding establishments in the Netherlands have a school on the premises. Boarders attend a 'regular' day school.

Not strict, not kind, ordinary, almost invisible as far as I was concerned. The school was new-build. Light, with everything visible and straightforward. You had your own desk in the classroom, with a separate chair. Not like the old school, with a desk for two and a lift-up lid as a writing surface. You could hide behind the lid and hide things underneath it. The old desk top contained a groove and an inkwell. We had such fun playing games – 'shooting' as we called it. You'd shoot wads of paper from the edge of the desk into the groove. The winner was the one who needed the fewest shots. I was the champion! The desk at the new school had a fixed writing surface with a fixed tray underneath where you could store things, but in full view. Far less interesting. You couldn't hide anything. Everything could be seen.. also by God. No groove, but a hole for an inkpot, though we used biros. I was good at school. This school was behind and so I was ahead. Unbelievable: I was one of the best in the class! That was bound to arouse suspicion. I did enjoy school. I was treated like a worthy person by those who taught us and it was evident among my fellow pupils. I wasn't considered stupid, not a 'lodger' though I was a 'boarder' as we were called – but there were more of them. At last at school I 'belonged'. I wasn't different, I was Sylvia! The nice thing about that school was that it wasn't attached to the convent, though middle school was. After breakfast you walked with a small group of children through the garden to school, unaccompanied by a nun. You played, like a 'normal' child, in the yard with 'non-boarders', children from the village. There was a difference: "you're a boarder", as a child can say in a contemptuous, unkind way, with a concomitant look.

So I had no problems at school, except with the gym teacher and the handwork sister, Hilda. She was also the nun at our boarding quarters during my recreation period and at bedtime. She thought I was smart – an idea she upheld in lessons, and so did I! The gym teacher was good-looking, as I recall. His wife also taught gym. She was slightly built and sharp-featured. She had black hair and a cranky expression. I was tall and well built for my age. I could feel the male teacher looking at me all the time and he often selected me out of a line to demonstrate something. We were always at variance with each other when I had to climb up the wall bars and do a bird's nest high up in the air. I was scared, feared heights. If I refused to do it I was sent out – a regular occurrence. Afterwards I'd be alone with him and notice him 'looking', but didn't understand at what. After a telling-off I was allowed to go. During Sister Carmelita's lessons in etiquette, also known as 'good manners', I learned that I should take care with strange men. They wanted only one thing, to abduct you. We didn't understand why, that wasn't explained. "They'll knock you out with a handkerchief doused in chloroform and then you'll be spirited away on a boat, never to return". That was the tale we were told. I wasn't really interested. There were boys and girls, so what!

When I was about 12 years old, just before I started my periods, my mother gave me a book with the title *May I look at myself when naked?* What a title! I always looked at myself in the mirror and laughed happily. I was no longer 'chubby' when I saw myself in my birthday suit! At boarding school I had to shower with the door open until I was seventeen. .. The pretext being that they, the nuns, could wash your back easily. They could keep an eye on you, to check you didn't do anything 'dirty', and they could ogle. One of the nuns said "How delicious you look!" I thought it sounded sordid, something she shouldn't say, but at that stage I didn't know who might make such a comment. I was ingenuous, but did sense what was right and what not. Then at least. And I still trusted my intuition, later on no more. I scarcely looked at mother's book. It also addressed menstruation. I leafed through it and when my mother returned (having left after giving it to me), I asked "Do boys have periods too?" My mother replied in the negative. How unfair – I do and they don't. I was angry. End of sex education! When at the convent I found blood in my underwear and a little later had stomach cramps, the only comment from the nun on duty was: "Just act as if it's nothing and you don't feel anything. Chin up, here is a sanitary towel with safety pins – fix it to your knickers." Acting as if there was nothing wrong was the way I was to behave with men later on, when I felt uncomfortable with them. I switched my feelings off and wasn't bothered. At least so I thought. "I'll act as if I don't notice or feel anything!"

Horrible, a huge piece of covered cardboard between your legs – that's what it felt like. The burning pain in your abdomen, the nasty smell, and pretending not to feel or smell anything. For me the world seemed to get crazier and crazier. But back to the lessons on manners. Table manners and rules of etiquette were taught as well, and rules that were convenient for 'them'. It was hard to get used to life in the actual boarding institution. Initially it was a matter of observing: who are the other children, can they be trusted, who is nice, who tells tales, who's who? Why are they here?

The odd thing is that you didn't have the real friendships that you had at a normal school. You're never together with your friend, you're always in a group and doing things in a group. For years I was 'allergic' to groups. I'm not keen on groups, I've had too many of them. I have not discovered that a group is safe – you're not safe from the group. Roles change easily. If you weren't a victim, but sided with the victim, you became one yourself. That's what's treacherous. Perhaps you were classified as nice one day, but the next day you could be a victim of a Maria sacrifice in the Maria grotto in the garden, or the butt of gossip. It was never my fate to land on the altar, but I was gossiped about. Looking back I wonder if I couldn't have done more to prevent it, that hell. I can envisage little Yvette, a skinny, pale, timid, almost translucent small girl. I never joined in actively and can't explain what led up to her being tied up, first to a tree and then on the Maria altar in the grotto. Pauline and Thea were the ringleaders. The nuns didn't 'see' what happened and you couldn't tell about it at home.

"Things like that don't happen", they'd say, "and otherwise you should tell the nun overseeing recreation". "She doesn't believe us", was my reply. Telling tales was definitely 'not on'. It was easier going to sleep. I'd cry myself to sleep and didn't need to check if my parents' pyjamas were in place. That fear proved to be deferred fear, it wasn't over, it grew. Who could say if they'd be at home when I returned? I had no contact with them and couldn't check. I still cry, it has always been my greatest fear, the trauma of being left in the lurch! I've actually left two long-term partners in the lurch myself. My feeling was that I had been abandoned, mentally. I couldn't do otherwise. It took a long time for me to take that step, aided by therapy to see if I wasn't mistaken. Others always knew better what was going on. Fortunately I sensed what wascorrect and what not, but I couldn't explain. Too scared … was I wrong, was I 'mistaken'? I still find it hard to distinguish whether it's me or the other. The answer is – ask! Nowadays I do. Perhaps too cautiously. "I don't want to be a nag", as my daughter recently said. Family karma? Somehow or other a child adapts.

Getting back to our boarding quarters after school, I obediently put on my pinafore, which hung in a fixed spot on a hook beside my coat. Your nameplate was next to the hook. When you put on your coat you took off your pinafore, and vice versa! My clothes were never dirty. On Sundays the coloured pinafore was exchanged for a white one. You were allowed clean clothes three times a week. For instance, clean underwear and socks, a different jumper to go with your skirt. The skirt was the same. We weren't allowed to wear trousers, I didn't even have any.

I had a couple of kilts in Scottish tartan, a couple of twinsets, twosets in brown mohair, stupid brown shoes, and a dress, alongside my blue Sunday uniform. You selected the clean clothes together with the nun in charge of the dormitory. No way could you have your own taste and you were monitored at all times. I like my own taste and no monitoring! Nowadays I even have my own fashion line. Sisters Carmelita and Hilda (who also taught handwork) were the nuns in charge of the dormitory and recreation. Sister Carmelita was also the head of the lower school, the 'juniors', as well as teaching etiquette. She was tall, slim, had a pretty face, dark hair. I also found her hypocritical. The way she prayed and walked, it appeared graceful, but I sensed it was artificial. She wasn't warm, unable to give, or receive,love. Otherwise she wouldn't have been in a convent. The first six weeks passed in a whirl. My parents came to collect my laundry one day and I was allowed to 'receive' them in the parlour. That's it – you talked to your parents as if they were strangers. I felt so uncomfortable in the parlour, there was distance between us, separated by a table. We were strangers. I cried even harder that night, my fear of abandonment increased. Before you knew, I'd become a nun too and never be allowed to leave! It was hard to understand. I could understand home life, it was my world which I could influence. Here I had no influence. My first weekend at home, after six weeks, was strange. I arrived in a strange house – where was home? Once more I had to keep quiet for my sister, my old friends had no time, no-one had time. Again I was living 'in between', midway, intruding. Between home and boarding school. I was getting to be too big for dolls, I couldn't share my grief with them. Babs' husband was always home during the weekend and then she was stuck with him and had no room for me. I'd lost that as well, my 'refuge'.

Fortunately I could visit Babs during the school holidays. Her children were at home and that was nice. We didn't speak about her cares any more. The children were around 7 and 4 years old, I think. Saskia and Anne. We resumed the sewing lessons, or else I larked around with the children. At the boarding establishment you had to keep your own cubicle clean: dusting, sweeping, beating out the rug, clean sheets, making up the bed. Every day there was some chore. When I was at home, instead of playing I cleaned my cold little room upstairs. Everything into the corridor, and then everything returned happily. I had a shelf above my bed for my dolls. Dolls from all over the world which my parents brought home with them from their travels, or else from our holidays in Austria or Switzerlandwith the Alpenkreuzer trailer tent. I cherished those dolls and often rearranged them. I haven't got them any more. I've never bought dolls like that for my children, nor have I encouraged them to buy them. I encouraged them to play doctors or hairdressers. Touching and caring for each other, that's what I prompted them to do. And I liked to be their patient or their customer. I was their best customer and always willing to play their game. Perhaps, with them, I made up for lost play time!I can't remember what games I played at boarding school. There wasn't much time. We often played out of doors in a little yard used by the kindergarten, where Sister Carmelita was in charge of the kindergarten during the day. We played with stilts, empty tin cans, making a hole in the bottom and passing a string through, then we could walk on them. It was great fun. I'll make them for my grandchildren later on. We also played tag with a ball, elastic twist with a skipping rope, chanting rhymes like 'salt, mustard, vinegar, pepper'. I remember a girl called Marthe, a friend of sorts. She had a huge bosom and when it was her turn to jump over the rope, her bosom bounced up and down – enormous! I was fascinated. Marthe didn't have a bra, nor did she have a father – no-one said anything about it, her mother was dead. She went to her mother's sister and her grandmother when we were allowed home. Marthe was miserable, grandmother and aunt were harsh. They didn't love her – she was worse off than me, I still had my sister and parents. I couldn't complain. Anyway, I was never allowed to complain, to crave something, not by anyone, certainly not in my last relationship. My relationship with Roel. "You've got everything your heart desires. You have and get everything you need, you just have to say the word and madam will get it!" I could hear my father saying that to my mother and thought: "Help!"

There were mornings when you were woken at 6.30 am,and others at 7 o'clock. The fluorescent lighting went on and a voice said: "Good morning girls. Time to get up". Then Carmelita or Hilda would walk past the cubicle curtains to see if you were out of bed. Outside your cubicle you would kneel down for morning prayers. On church days, wearing your coloured hat, you'd go off to mass. There were altar boys – almost the only boys you saw and that was exciting. I thought they were pious and virtuous. Hmmmmm! After mass, or else straight from the dormitory to the refectory for breakfast. Sister Maria went round with a big urn of lukewarm, watery tea.

For breakfast, there was often brawn, black pudding and 'scouring powder' – sugar mixed with cocoa – nice and cheap and it tasted good – and cheese cut so thinly you could almost see through it. There was white and brown factory-made bread. The senior at the table had to check that you first took sliced meat, only after that was 'scouring powder' permitted. Once, a few years later, I was the senior. Only for a very short time … we had too much fun at my table, no table manners. I can laugh about it… we had competitions to see who could eat the most bread. I was the champion, with 12 slices! Shooting peas, like balls of paper, was another favourite – again, I was often the winner. My report, something we got once a month for conduct, discipline, neatness, politeness and table manners, was a different matter. Champion in being the worst! I didn't care, I was proud of my resistance. It was the only bit of being 'human'. I felt as if I was still myself thanks to that poor report. It proved to be an illusion. My basic trust in the feeling that I mattered and meant something, began to fall apart. But as a young girl, I didn't yet realise it. The realization came later and then twice as hard. Of course, with a good school report I went on to the next class, with Sister Priscilla as my teacher.One thing was certain: I would leave boarding school at the end of the year. The MULO (comparable with middle school) wasn't an option. My future lay at the Edith Stein Lyceum in The Hague – back home! Meanwhile some things had changed in the convent. The nuns had no more blue material for the uniforms and uniform was abolished. The boarding part was modernised. The nuns continued to wear their wimples, but they were allowed to leave their necks bare. The mass and church service were different too. The priest now faced the congregation. That was a big change, and we girls were now allowed to take it in turns to be altar servers.

We had a new girl at our boarding school, Yoze. We became friends – and are again, even after an interval of thirty years. We were always there for each other, in our hearts, loyal as we are. Yoze had two big sisters and two small brothers. She was 'in between', and her parents hoped she would stand out more at boarding school. Now, a little less than 50 years later, we still call each other sisters. After two years Yoze emigrated to California. With the whole family, plus five brothers and a sister of her father's, and all their children. They were all horticulturalists in the Dutch 'Westland', an area known for its greenhouse horticulture. They wanted to expand, grow more varieties of tomatoes and flowers, have bigger houses, and in the Netherlands there was no room for growth. Just rules to prevent it. Perhaps (well, perhaps) little has changed in that respect. Their emigration meant I lost yet another friend. YET AGAIN! Yoze is very ill now, she has cancer with metastases. She still lives in California. When she emigrated we wrote to each other. When she was 17 she came to stay with me. I was living back home again, but in a bigger house, albeit in a different building, a small apartment. We travelled with my father for a month through what was then Yugoslavia. My father slept in the car and we in a tent. Yoze was sturdy and I was slim. Anorexia was setting in, though it wasn't yet apparent. A year later – I'd earned 2,000 guilders cooking after school for an old lady and her sick daughter – I visited Yoze for a month. By then I had anorexia. Today we see each other regularly, using Skype. We love each other dearly and fortunately each time our final farewell is delayed. We've now agreed to arrange a special farewell for each other before the time has come. Our 'physical' farewell. We'll also have Edith Piaf songs played and sing along with them for each other: "non, je ne regrette rien". We talked recently about our childhood friendship. What was going on, what we admired about each other. I thought Yoze was funny, a small, blond, gutsy girl, with full lips, quick-tempered, standing up for herself. And we could have fun together, fooling round, as we called it. Yoze admired me for supporting her loyally though thick and thin, whatever the consequences. Apparently she once pushed Kitty into the mud when they were playing. Not on purpose, but the nuns implied everything we did was on purpose. I organised a garden hose and sprayed Kitty down – all traces of mud disappeared! I know, I wasstill 'self-assured' and fully endorsed what I did. Whether I was punished or not, I was never frightened, only proud. I never lied. Yoze and I met up again after 30 years through of a reunion of Sister Priscilla's primary school class. It was in 2008. At the time I was in Croatia with Roel, my ex-partner, whom I left, physically, early in 2011. I'd left him much earlier, emotionally. In my mailbox I found an announcement of the reunion: "Hereby a request to Sylvia Duijm from Yoze. If Sylvia Duijm will attend the reunion, so will I!" I met Yoze at Schiphol airport. I'd never heard of the television programme 'Hello, Goodbye', but the crew was there and our reunion was filmed! An important document for me. All of a sudden I was 'famous'. In shops, even in Africa, at Banjul airport, a woman came up to me and asked: "Weren't you on TV, in 'Hello, Goodbye'?" How wonderful to feel, to know that my childhood friendship with Yozealready consisted of love and loyalty. I can draw on an experience around which life revolves. Love and loyalty. Today Yoze is learning a lot about herself in her own relationship. The other party would seem not to be strong enough to support her and alleviate her suffering. I wonder whether we choose partners who are less strong than we are? Partners who do not dare to go through fire, but perhaps through a tea-light candle?

Rules at boarding school became less strict. You were allowed home every weekend. Pinafores were done away with, but not hats yet. I never managed to go home every weekend. I sometimes had to stay at school as a punishment. We'd agreed to run away from Sister Maria who took us on a walk on the beach every Wednesday afternoon. Incredible: we walked in crocodile through the village, at such a slow pace, you felt like a dog being let out. But dogs like to run away. And all of a sudden we flew off. Sister Maria of the cleft palate couldn't shout very easily. And we pretended not to hear. The punishment was harsh. Because of Sister Maria's disability we had to spend the weekend at school. I think in the 6 years I was there I had to stay behind 12 times. I didn't mind too much. Weekends at home were dull. I didn't have any friends left in The Hague. I hoped to make friends again once I attended the Edith Stein Lyceum. Sister Priscilla was satisfied and suggested I attend a lyceum. The other children in my class were destined either for a domestic science school or middle school. I was different. I was from the city and of a different class. I had to do the entrance exam at the Edith Stein Lyceum. I encountered my old friend Maaike (father a doctor). I was so pleased, I had the start of new friendships. I found the exams easy. My best mark proved to be 5 out of 10. You attended 'trial lessons' all week. I was living at home again for just a week. It was hard, but right away there was a teacher I thought was very 'nice'- the maths teacher. But I didn't like his subject. And then came a second time at boarding school that I almost fainted, life just drained out of me. My parents came to see me, unannounced. I can still weep at the thought. I went happily to the parlour, my parents were there! I entered and saw, especially from my father's face: "I've got bad news for you. You didn't pass, you won't be going to the Edith Stein Lyceum. You'll have to do middle school and continue to board here, it's too far to travel to and fro." I flew into my father's arms, wanting comfort, love, what else? I don't remember . Life just stood still for a moment. The next day I was allowed to ring Maaike. I got her irritated father on the phone. When I told him I wanted to tell Maaike I'd failed, he replied: "Oh, all right", with not a sign of sympathy. Yet another doctor who ignored emotions! I was to meet a whole lot more. Later I heard that my father had tried to get me into a boarding establishment with a secondary school. My mother wanted me home, and just go to middle school in The Hague – my father didn't consider it to be the right environment. I stayed on at the convent.

Grandmother, who lived next door to us, became increasingly ill and never went outside any more. She stayed in bed and my mother spent a lot of time with her. My mother was extremely fond of her, and she of my mother. Also my mother always accompanied grandma to hospital for her radiation treatment. They discussed a lot of things with each other. Occasionally grandma could be truculent with my father. Mother wanted a television set, father didn't. Grandmother bought one for my mother, a white portable set, which my father didn't have to watch. Grandma always waved to me as I left for boarding school on a Sunday evening. She'd push the curtain aside and I could see her look, saying "if it were up to me you'd be at home near me". Also if, unusually, my mother took me on the back of her bike to the bus station on a Monday morning I'd see grandma push aside the curtain and wave to me. She and I understood each other. When I started at middle school things changed again. There were boys in my class, different teachers and then I was one of the 'big ones'. By then I was having piano lessons, actually for two years already, singing and acting lessons, there was enough distraction. I still wasn't happy. Still alone. I slept in the big dormitory, an enormous room, and I was becoming a real adolescent. Pimples, and insecure about my face and body. Every morning the horrible fluorescent lighting went on and the pimples in my face looked even worse. My body changed even more. By then I had a bra, a Playtex 'Cross your heart'. Purchased at a specialist shop in The Hague. They measured your breasts and you were 'packed in'. I had a bra far sooner than my sister. I was an 'early developer', as it was called. I was fascinated by my changing body. Before the lights were switched off, I explored. I saw hairs round my pussy. I saw a kind of white cream at my labia, and that was new. It was different and smelled special. Sometimes I tasted it, another time I played around a bit. Just a voyage of discovery, how I was made. One day I was leaving the dormitory when I heard "dirty pig, slob, ugh! how mucky you are". The words I'd used for Anneke as I followed her through town when we were in Miss Terstraat's class, were now being used for me. The difference being that not one girl, but three girls were saying them. I'd done nothing wrong. The rest only had to say 'slob' and I'd be cut dead for a month for my behaviour. Apparently Thea, my neighbour in the next cubicle, had spied on me. She and Pauline thought up the punishment. The two of them had also been responsible for the sacrifice on the Maria altar. Yoze was no longer at school to help me. I was all alone and dared tell no-one. It heralded my denial of my womanhood. I remember that if, when I was 5 or 6 we went for a family walk in a park or wood and saw a couple kissing, I'd say: "stupid, when I see people kissing I need to go to the loo". My mother's answer would invariably be "Don't be silly!" I was merely a healthy child with the right feeling in the right place. When I was home I liked nothing better than to read Jan Wolkers' book *A Rose of Flesh* before dinner. I thought the scene in which he slapped her bottom as she walked up the stairs as well as when she was on the bed, and her buttocks turned red and soft like jelly, was great. It made me hungry, a rush of dopamine! I'd lock myself in the loo opposite the dining room. My sister realised what was going on and gave me away. That too was forbidden. None of it was allowed, you had to deny that area, front and back. I took heed. I enjoyed school. Lots of nice day pupils. At the convent I made sandwiches for break time with filling I didn't like. I swapped them with various pupils whose mothers made delicious sandwiches for me. I gave them my packet to throw away in their bin at home. I was once caught out when my sandwiches were found somewhere in a dustbin. A strict eye was kept on us.

Three sisters joined our boarding school – Ankie, Jozette and Antonia. Antonia was in the class above me and we became friends. The girls, there were seven children in the family, were from The Hague. Their father worked in occupational training and their mother was a real businesswoman, she had set up two shops selling office supplies with two of her children, Jaap and Joyce. She often went to auctions as well, and bought a lot of antiques. She recognised what was valuable or might become more valuable. She didn't spend a lot of time on her children. Antonia's maternal grandmother lived with them. She took care of them a lot and Antonia didn't like it. The ties between Antonia and me were mainly on account of 'being naughty' and perhaps, unconsciously, because "they don't like us". Antonia was small and very slim. She had a high voice and was somewhat anxious. I was never anxious or fearful, not when getting up to pranks – then I was entirely myself. I remember it well. I'd asked my mother to put some gingerbread in my bag because it works as a laxative. She did. In fact, it was intended to make 'diarrhoea' which I spread with cotton buds on the toilet seat and bowl in the teachers' and pupils' loos. I'd come up with the idea and Antonia had to help me. The students' toilets were ready. Now to the staff room. Unfortunately, the maths teacher, Mr. Van Driel, who used to call me 'the flavour of the month', wanted to use the toilet. We were in there! He waited outside. At some stage we emerged and ran off with our bucket. We rushed into a classroom and hid in the cupboard. Before long we heard a shrill cry: "Where are you?" It was the headmistress, Sister Germania. She wore spectacles with blurred lenses as if they were steamed up – and she was looking for us. The cupboard door opened and there we were. What a scream! "What cheeky, rude children you are to do something like this." Punishment and a weekend spent at school. That strengthened the bond between Antonia and me. We had to do a whole lot more school work. The nun who supervised us while we did our work was Sister Germaine. She was really nice. She had a kind, understanding look and she smuggled in goodies for us. I can just see her, sitting there. Healthy, rosy cheeks, brown eyes and a naughty look. She'd been young herself, and still was, in her dreams. We also had extra chores: cleaning the chapel windows and other cleaning duties. I do remember we had a good time, better for me than at home, where nothing happened. At school I attracted a lot of attention, especially from the boys in the class. I never understood why. They even touched me. I had good taste and had more and more input about what I wore. By then I had a larger cubicle in which there was room for a cupboard. I liked to wear knitted clothes, still do. They show your figure, your shape to advantage. I remember that when I was 8 years old if my dress had a bow at the back I wanted it tied very tight, to show off my waist. Everyone in the family thought I was crazy and no-one helped out – to my annoyance. I'd stamp my feet and my mother would try again, to satisfy me. We had to go to church and she didn't want to arrive late – and I knew. In church, I linked arms with her, to hold close to my mother for a moment. She'd shake me off. I always felt she found it awkward to be on display like that in church.

Back to boys. I got on well with them. Most girls were concerned with girly things, like dyeing their hair, using tanning lotion and make-up, as well as falling in love and exhibiting hysterical girlish behaviour. I wanted to laugh, move around, have fun. Boys thought the same, apart from their secret fantasies when they clung to my dress at certain places. At school I got on well with the teachers and that was reflected in my marks. The better I got on with them, the more effort I made and the better the marks. For German I got an 8 from Mr. Huiskens. His mother took over the lessons and considered me to be a 'fishwife' because I could be rather noisy. My mark then was a 4. Incredible. And my lower marks were taken seriously, as if I'd suddenly lost my brain.

Back home at the weekend. On Fridays I'd take the bus home and on Sunday evenings back to school by car. One time my father took Antonia and me, and we collected her at her house. Another time her brother Jaap took us. When he was born, Jaap suffered a deficiency of oxygen and it meant he was a bit odd. He was a loner, and talked to himself. But he was a dear. We had great fun with him when he drove us to school. Once he made a detour through the red-light district of The Hague. It became a tradition when Jaap drove us. The three of us had a great time. The women, the atmosphere, you knew what it was about, and yet you didn't… I was very curious about what went on there, and the clothing the women wore. Exciting. You could see everything that you could envisage under my brown, knitted dress. To add to the fun, we rang the bells of the teachers' houses, and then Jaap drove us off at speed! Fantastic, I can feel the excitement and fun again today. The best outing of the week. We were very fond of Jaap. Our secret.

My sister attended the Edith Stein Lyceum, three forms above me because I'd stayed down a year and also had a 'late' birthday. She had a friend called Hellen. There were twelve children in that family and they lived in a huge house. It had twelverooms and at one time it had been a bishop's residence. There was a fireplace in the vast hall. Occasionally I went along with my sister to Hellen's. There were so many children and I got on well with Alex. He was a year older and was at Aloysius College, run by priests. On Saturday evenings Hellen and Alex sometimes came to our house and we played records in the sun room. Now and then. We also went with our parents to visit the De Wit family. They were very old friends and we were old enough to tag along. They had a huge villa. They had two children, one of whom, Angela, also suffered anoxia at birth, and Fons. Angela was strange, she went to a special school, and Fons was shy. If I asked him something he blushed bright red. We watched TV, played a game, drank lemonade and were given crisps. At midnight we went home. We celebrated New Year's Eve with the Boot family. Also, I saw my childhood friend, Stef, the boy next door in New Guinea, growing up, because, though we were no longer friends, we met up because of our parents. He had become shy and I didn't think he was interesting. However, my parents lost all their friends. There wassomething wrong with all of them. My father blamed it on the other people, he found fault with everyone. My parents were incapable of investing in friendships. For that you need compassion and love, and must be prepared to open up to others. They showed the outside world what was 'proper', appealing, cold, and *comme il faut*.

In the weekends there were more 'distractions' from outside. I played tennis with Antonia on Saturdays and met up with Pitty there. Everything seemed a bit more carefree. However, grandma's health was deteriorating further. I remember coming home one Friday evening and she was worse:she had been admitted to hospital. My sister and I visited her there. She could no longer speak and I don't know if she was aware that I was with her to say 'hello' and tell her how much I loved her. Grandma died that night. My sister and I were the last to see her. At last we were allies. We'd experienced something of importance together. It was very hard to say farewell to grandmother. No more pushing the curtain aside. Her house had to be sold and her sister, Dien, had to go into a care home. All grandma's belongings had to be sold, including our house. Later, my father told us he wanted to buy the house but uncle Jacques (mother's brother) didn't want that . Nothing, none of the possessions, were to stay in the family.

Meanwhile Antonia's dissatisfaction with boarding school had become apparent. She had tried to get a letter out via one of the day pupils and it was intercepted. In addition, she arranged a 'midnight' get-together in the dormitory so we could watch fireworks. She was expelled. They thought she was underhand. I was often caught, but not expelled. Where was I better off? It proved too problematical for Antonia to travel by bus back and forth every day, and she changed schools. Yet another supportive friend gone from the boarding establishment. We'd had a good bond and now I was alone. No more fooling around. . I felt very much alone, I was so different. The girls at the convent were primarily those who 'went too far' with boys and so had to be 'watched'. They talked only about their figure, clothes, make-up and hair extensions, which were 'in'. I thought it was stupid and felt very lonely. The Sunday evening drive to boarding school was gloomy again. No-one spoke much in the car. My father bade me an awkward farewell. Every week he sent me a postcard depicting Rotterdam, telling what he was doing and how things were at home. Quite something – sending a card of Rotterdam every week for at least 4 years, school holidays excepted. He always sent the card from work and always signed it 'your loving father'. I was very pleased to receive the cards, they arrived on Wednesdays. My father was the only child in his family who hadn't been to boarding school. The sister who preceded him in age died when she was 3 months old. My father came after her and that grandmother (the one of 'hands on top of the blanket' and the high pyjama bottoms), wanted a child at home with her – that was my father. There were six children altogether, including Flora. Another two followed my father – Ria and Albert. I don't think grandmother would have had children if it hadn't been part of her faith. It remains a mystery to me that she ever opened her legs to receive grandpa's seed! As a good Catholic, you were expected to produce children. My father told us that his father had said, when he was an adolescent: "I sometimes feel like poking your mother's eyes out, then at least she won't see anything any more". Grandmother was concerned solely with controlling and enforcing how others were supposed to behave. She was also a diabetic and she exploited it in order to get others to do her bidding. My father had grown up without love. He longed to have a woman's lap to sit on. My mother was also cool and prudish, and was unable to give him the warmth he sought. My sister describes my father as oversexed. I don't agree. When something is beyond your reach you long for it all the more. My father often longed for the comfort and breasts of their mutual acquaintances. My parents moved house many times, even in their later years, and they would be helped by someone from the church, usually a single lady. She would become friendly with my parents, my father in particular. More about that later.

So Antonia was no longer at school and every Wednesday afternoon I had the opportunity to talk to the mentor. He was our spiritual father. So strange – I was around 15 years of age, a woman to all appearances, yet it was customary for me to sit on his lap. Without reservations, his hands round my middle, nice and safe. I've absolutely no idea what we spoke about. After half an hour I'd leave, with 25 cents, and was allowed through a secret door to go into the village to buy a bag of chips. I believe I was the only one who was so favoured. At boarding school they kept you in your place. The other girls came to boarding school when they were older. I was already almost a nun by then and knew nothing about adolescence – an ongoing trauma. I still enjoyed playing outdoors. The village had acquired a cinema and we were taken there once a month. Every evening you had to take a vitamin pill. Once I stood up and said: "if I don't swallow this pill, things could go badly for me" – alluding to 'the pill'. I was aware of that and that time was not allowed to go to the cinema with the others. However, what was allowed was for the nuns to see you naked in the morning and say "how delicious you look" or else during folk dancing they could hold your hand longer than necessary. I disliked it all and decided to act as if I didn't notice. Just act as if you've heard nothing, felt nothing, noticed nothing. Just deny it. That's the way I behaved with men later on. I got better at it.

I fell in love with Alex, one of twelve children. He had a cool, green raincoat, a parka; he also had a Puch moped. He had a cheeky look and was simply nice. He came to collect me from boarding school on his Puch and I said he was my cousin. They believed me and I was allowed to show him round. Wow, I was so proud – my cousin Alex. He thought I was cool, being at boarding school, and didn't mind I was at middle school. Yet I did feel a bit inferior. At home they considered me to be stupid – and they told me so. When my parents had visitors, my sister and I would join them for a while. My sister recounted her successes at school and I was allowed to tell of my antics at boarding school. I was 'Binny with the pinny'. The pinafore I wore at boarding school. When I grew up, I'd be a mother and have lots of children, and that was good enough for me. My sister was to go on to university. By then I was having dancing lessons from Mr. Kuipers. The royal princesses had had dancing lessons from him too. In fact, I wasn't supposed to because I was at middle school and that was inferior. My father's job – accountant – and our higher social class were reasons to make an exception. I was the only middle school pupil and the tallest girl in the group. The boys liked me, I was never a wallflower. And again, the dancing teacher picked me out to demonstrate steps with him. I wore knee socks, but he wanted me to wear stocking. The first time I did, they were real tights and, after dancing for 5 minutes I got a ladder in them!

By then we'd moved house again, to an apartment that was far too small. Our old house had been sold. My sister was living in rooms, or else was about to, and so did I, later. When we reached the age of 18 my father thought we should live on our own. Good for our independence. When I was in the fourth form and at home for the weekend, I had a serious accident on the way back from the dentist. I was riding the little moped I'd paid for myself – known as the 'girl's Puch'. It was December and it got dark early. It was Friday evening, cold, and I wanted to get home fast. At the beginning of the street there was a 'no entry' sign. I thought I could manoeuvre through on my moped. I hadn't realised,or saw too late, that there was no way through, and I landed with a crash in a hole. With part of the tram rails in my stomach and abdomen and another part piercing my thighs. The first thing I shouted whenfelt the severe pain in my abdomen was: "I'll never be able to have children!" And then I fainted. In and out of consciousness from the pain. In hospital I pleaded with the doctor to kill me. The pain was unbearable, and I can stand a lot of pain. X-rays, throwing up over everything with pain. The X-rays revealed nothing. By then my parents were worried stiff. They only discovered that I was in hospital a few hours after I'd been admitted. I had no means of identification on me. They went to the police station to make enquiries. My parents were looking for me. At 2 a.m. they were rung for permission to cut me open. I wouldn't survive otherwise, my blood pressure was life-threateningly high. I was the miracle of that hospital. My liver, spleen, everything was ruptured. My abdomen and stomach filled with blood. They welded and repaired me everywhere they could, and my female organs ... untouched! I spent a week in hospital, in a ward with 40 patients. In the end I looked a bit like Snow White, with a glass casket covering me. There was a complication: pneumonia. I thought the doctors were handsome, one in particular, and when I saw him I blushed even redder than my high temperature warranted. I wanted to walk out of hospital as a 'woman'. I'd asked my mother to bring a particular skirt and pair of shoes as I knew I looked great in them. She brought a child's dress and knee socks. I left hospital, defeated. Back home I had to regain my strength before returning to boarding school. Mother had got a cake and there we sat, in silence, facing each other. We had nothing to say. She said: "That's nice, have another slice". I felt so lonely, with that stranger. A week later I was allowed back to school. With a cushion in my back, no greasy food and no sudden movement, quiet. I'd told my cousin Christa, who sometimes stayed with us and was a nurse at one of the hospitals in The Hague, something about my crush on Alex. She wanted to know a whole lot about him. Once I went with him to a party at his school. When I was dancing with Rolf, who was in the same dance class as me, I felt something hard against my pubis. I thought he had something in his trouser pocket! I knew nothing. At boarding school we read *Tina*, a weekly magazine for young girls, and we watched children's films. Then my cousin 'pinched' Alex – she seduced him and he let it happen, while I was at boarding school. It was very hurtful, mean, unfair, sly!

After middle school, I was supposed to go to the HAVO (senior general secondary education). Every Wednesday evening during the last six months, I went with Mariska, a day girl, for chemistry lessons at the Aloysius College. It was an outing for me. The teacher, Mr. De Greef, turned out to be the father of Yoze De Greef, who was to become my friend at a later stage. At that teacher's home I discovered what it was like for a man and a woman to love each other. When he got home from work his wife would be waiting for him at the front door as soon as she heard his key in the lock. He'd pick her up and carry her to the bedroom, where they took their time for a loving 'hello'. That's what I wanted later. And later is now! When my great love arrives, I stand at the lift and we are together, for each other, all the way. A deep, intense greeting that we continue in my little house! Splendid. Thank you, Mr. and Mrs. De Greef!

Boarding school behind me, returning twice. The first time with my boyfriend, Sjaak. The boarding school had gone, it was a rest home for old nuns, the last time with Roel, my ex. The convent and boarding school had been converted into apartments, the chapel was now a kind of library, and the refectory a 'common room'. The garden, the Maria altar, had been replaced with new-build. The staircase up to what used to be the sleeping cubicles was still intact. All that was left. How often did that little, woebegone Sylvia walk up and down those stairs weeping, longing for loving care.

My next school, Sint Jans College, was for boys and girls near Kijkduin, a beach resort near The Hague, and

I lived some three miles away on the border with Scheveningen. The school had an experimental section in accordance with the latest secondary education act ('Mammoetwet'). I was admitted into the fourth form of the HAVO. I'd stayed down once before at primary school, and now for the second time here. Tall, yet still a child! I became friends with Tim, the brother of Roel, my ex. Tim smoked dope and was miserable at home, as I was. The atmosphere, his parents, they were just the same as my own. His father was an accountant and his mother was weary and bilious – even worse than mine! Tim was always stoned, I didn't really know what it was. He had some land belonging to his parents close to where the now king Willem-Alexander and his wife Maxima live in Wassenaar. He had chickens there, as well as a horse and covered wagon. My parents forbade me to go round with Tim and in the end it was bound to happen. Tim had left home and school too, and I found him increasingly difficult to understand. He was the first boy I allowed to touch my breasts. We were sitting in my room, playing a record of The Doors. I found it exciting and pleasant, with his hands stroking my warm breasts. We kissed too. All of a sudden, he'd gone. Roland was another friend, a real Tory type. If you asked him for a light, he'd present you with a matchbox with the party logo on it. I started smoking and smoked 'roll-your-owns' with Samson tobacco and Rizla Blue rolling papers. Roland smoked a pipe. Tim and Roland hung out together because of me! Amusing, the two extremes. They were both from well-to-do families, Roland's was an old money family. His parents thought I was acceptable on account of my father's profession and the street where I lived in The

Hague. We kept in touch for a long time. Later I often stayed with him when I was working in Rotterdam, where he lived. Roland wanted to marry me. That caused the friendship to wane. I wasn't attracted to him physically, nor did I envisage myself as a 'hostess' in his successful career. He has a big family, his wife is also an orthopedagogue, he's happy and now lives in Belgium.

I also had a girlfriend, Maria, from a family with eight children. Maria and I got on well. In the early days she often came to my place to study, in my large bedroom. When we took a break we put on soul music and danced, delightfully in front of the mirror. I discovered later that Sister Huberta, my last headmistress, was her aunt. The world's a funny old place! Maria had a brother, Siem – one of her many brothers. He liked me. He was studying medicine in Leiden. He came round to my parents to ask if I might go with him to one of the student parties. It was permitted and I was allowed to sleep over. Not in his bed. We'd kissed sometimes and walked with his arm round me. I was proud. Siem had a big hawk nose and a pointed face. Very humorous, tall and quick-witted. Things I like. I don't remember a lot about the party. He slept on the floor and I in his bed. The following morning I went shopping and bought a whole bag of food for him: 'student's food'. Caring and not seductive. He took me to the station and waved me off. The following weekend I was at Maria's and Siem wanted to talk to me. It was 'off'. I was very upset, because, you know, I wasn't nice enough…

One day I returned home from school and my parents had tidied and altered my room. My bed had feet under it, my records were in a cupboard, everything that was recognisably mine, because it meant something to me, had gone. My world collapsed. Even my room had been taken away from me and it was all I had. My safe, pretty, little house. My father used to say: "Nothing is yours, everything is mine because I paid for it". I shut myself away and at some stage I fled to Maria's, to my better mother. She understood me, but said: "I don't have any room, you can't sleep here". And what did stupid Siem say: "She can lie in bed with me!" Rejection and attraction, double messages, I was so familiar with them. Tears poured down my cheeks. Maria's mother rang my parents and I was allowed to do my own thing again. That was that, I couldn't go on. Not long ago Yoze in America showed me a letter I wrote her at the time" "Hi, dear Yoze, I think it's silly, but the doctor says I'm stressed out…, 17 years old and stressed out! He thinks I should take some time off." Now I understand why. I was so tired. Maria had decided she wanted to lose weight and I, with the persistent trauma of being 'chubby' and what my father called 'footballer's knees', plus my damaged self-image, decided I should too. I had to take care with fat and alcohol because of my damaged liver, I had a weapon. No-one could force me to eat. But I kept going. In the end I weighed 44 kilos, even though I'm 1.77 metres tall (today I weigh between 60 and 62 kilos). I had my hair cut short, something I never wanted to do, and began wearing dresses with puff sleeves. I refused to eat,became isolated – when you visited people you had to eat and drink. I got my school-leaving certificate and, when it was presented to me (wearing my puff-sleeved dress), I was complimented for having succeeded, with good marks even, despite my ruptured liver. They hadn't a clue, any of them!

I went to Yoze and her family in California for the summer holidays. Paid for out of my own earnings. I was proud about that money. I'd always had jobs, ever since I was sixteen, and was able to buy what I thought was pretty. They were horrified at how little was left of me!

Denying my womanhood

I spent a wonderful month in California. At last I was part of a family, and treated as such. I was given attention, I felt love and I was told how things were done in this family – I felt I was seen and loved. Aunt Riet, Yoze's mother, treated me as her own child: sincerely, bluntly. I allowed her to see a vulnerable, damaged girl – the exterior – and I thought I was revealing a tough Sylvia, because deep down that's how I wanted to feel, longing for that once strong, fine child. I fell in love with Yoze's brother Wil – something I confessed to him three years ago, when I was visiting Yoze. He was unsure of himself, of his relationship, and now a 'beautiful, strong' woman was prepared to tell him that, to comfort him. I so wanted him to have a more healthy image of himself. I am very aware of what an unhealthy self-image can do to you!

I don't know how he felt about me when I was an adolescent, I didn't ask him. It's not important. The only thing to spoil that holiday was the fact that my wisdom teeth were playing up. They had to be extracted surgically. I barely ate, I was so scared of getting fat. 'My liver' following the traffic accident, continued to be my 'weapon'.

I hardly dared to clean my teeth, for fear of ingesting water! I did clean them, but apprehensively. That subject's worthy of an entire book, if only to help an outsider understand the mindset and deep-rooted fears of an anorexia patient. I would also like to help heal patients with a book of that type. That book, my book, will be written. I already know its title: 'Help, water makes me fat'. I had to cure myself, because at that time anorexia was an unknown.

The month had passed, back to Holland! I was destined to become a nurse, though I wanted to study the Dutch language or interior design. Too ambitious for 'Minny with her pinny', at least that's what my parents said. Father Niekus, my Dutch teacher, recognised my talent. Moreover, having made all manner of alterations to my room, I had developed a greater interest in the ideal living surroundings.

Yet my stays in hospital (three times in two years due to my ruptured liver) made me keen to become a nurse, if accepted. By then I was 18, almost 19: time to leave home. I went to Delft, for my in-service nursing training at Bethel Hospital. The admission procedure was bizarre. The medical director conducted the physical examination personally. A short interview followed by a medical, consisting of undressing down to your underpants (nowadays your panties!). I had to do some unusual gymnastic exercises, many of which might be what you'd expect in a nightclub! It was somewhat reminiscent of my gym teacher at the School of the Sacred Heart – the way I was 'observed'. I didn't dare refuse. I didn't actually know if it was strange, and I was scared I wouldn't be accepted, weighing 44 kilos. It turned out I was the only one who had to perform the contortions. Today it would be called abuse of power – a person in a position of power, such as a senior medical officer, taking advantage of someone in that way.(Me-Too, Avant la lettre.)

I had a small room in the nurses' home. The other residents included police trainees and a few students. My room contained Pastoe (modern) furniture, which I put on top of the cupboard and replaced with my own familiar belongings – my life and my taste. They included the small wooden 'potty chair' with a lid that I used as a child. We weren't allowed to remove any of the original furniture from the room so it was very full. Ank lived next door to me. She had been going out with Evert for two years. He was studying aeronautical engineering. They're still together and are just as happy, or even happier than in those early days. Ank and I became friends. We met up again last year and follow each other on Facebook. Marly lived there too. She was going out with Henk, he was at the Royal Military Academy (KMA)And they too are still together and we also follow each other on Facebook. I didn't have a boyfriend as such, though I did have a very special relationship with Andries, who was an architecture student and also lived in the same block of flats. Andries had a steady girlfriend. I loved him and he loved me. We saw each other every day and we were very open and loving together (though not sexually). He knew what was going on with me. He was the catalyst that made me put my anorexia behind me. We had a party in the nurses' home and Andries went with me. While we danced together he said: "I'm very fond of you, crazy about you, but it's upsetting to hold you like this, I scared of breaking you". That was dreadful – he being frightened to hold me! I did so want to be held by him in the way of a good friend, a pal, for comfort and support, confirming our close friendship. The next day I made an appointment with the internist, I could barely keep food down any more. He referred me to a dietician. It took at least four years for me to recover fully. To know anorexia no longer had a hold over me, that I was free. I only really enjoyed food after some time.

Nursing proved not to be for me. However, the loving care for and contact with patients certainly were. They loved me and wanted me at their bedside. My great competitors, the senior nurses, forced me to do all the chores that kept me out of sight and in the washing-up kitchen. Reminiscent of Miss Terstraat! The lack of independence was another drawback – you always carried a notebook with you and, once you had performed a certain number of tasks, someone signed it. Not my cup of tea! I was too astute, noticed too much but wasn't allowed to report it: as a trainee you're 'stupid'. I wanted to get away. I was allowed to go on living in the nurses' home, had a variety of office and hospitality jobs. All in The Hague. Including working for Ennia, an insurance company, in the typing pool. There were six women, all older, 'real' women. We were allowed to go to the lavatory every two hours: I went for that reason, they to touch up their hair and make-up. I liked it there and chattered away. The outcome was a 'place of honour' beside the boss…. Then I kept quiet. I also worked at the Bijenkorf department store in The Hague, in the restaurant. When there were foreigners, the boss called me. I spoke various languages, he didn't! I thought it was awful, wore clothes that were too large, I was still too skinny for the Bijenkorf uniform. I didn't want to wait at tables looking like that or to be brought in specially. Being paid attention, wearing an oversized uniform! I definitely did not feel like a hostess or a woman.

So, what then? My parents had decided that I should study for my teaching certificate – the 'Akte NXX'. Never heard of it! It transpired that it trained you for child care and crafts. With the certificate I would easily find work and have school holidays with my own – future –children. Meanwhile my father had purchased a large apartment in The Hague where I could live as the main tenant, with other tenants occupying the third floor. Very nice. A small avenue with romantic lampposts and a canal in front. The apartment was large, I had my own dressing room adjoining my street-side bedroom. By then I had more clothes, shoes, bags than anyone else – paid for out of my own earnings. I created a farmhouse setting. The windows were small, it was very snug after the Spartan atmosphere at Bethel Hospital. My father gave me a free hand and he and his brother Albert, plus 'proper' workmen, did a great deal. My mother was often there, for instance to steady a ladder. Something unusual happened with my father, something I'll always cherish – as with more things about my father. After I'd been there a week or two, I rang home in tears, I wanted to live at home again. My father said: "Syl, of course you can come home if you want. Think about it carefully and take time to get used to your new place. Sleep on it for a couple of nights.". That's exactly what the 'love of my life' would say!

The NXX programme. Amazingly I encountered Maaike again. For the third time. First in Miss Terstraat's class, then at the Edith Stein Lyceum, and now again. We didn't renew our friendship, but we did join forces on a project that was a kind of traineeship. Youth centre activities for potential young delinquents. We made a good team. I could sense what they needed and Maaike, who was calm, could explain things well. I was too enthusiastic! Maaike possessed calmness and authority, I was still too much one of them.

I hated the actual course of study, so girlish, so scholastic. I wanted to leave, go to the college for social studies – there you had freedom! My parents arranged for a test, but the advice was still NXX. I was said to have managerial qualities, so all would be well! Life at my house got better and better. Hilarious – Bert, who worked at Ennia (though I never saw him there) came to live with us. We often had 'meetings with chairman Heineken and chairman Bols', our euphemism. My liver wasn't playing up any more, I needed 'the weapon' less and less and we had a whale of a time at our meetings. It did result in my skipping college from time to time: to recuperate. I felt free. We had one shower and when Bert and I were in a rush, we showered together. Also, I took him coffee in bed almost daily. We didn't have sex, but friendship, and we cherished each other. We were goofy together. One time I bought a wedding dress in the Maison Petite sale in The Hague. Together with Antonia, with whom I'd got up to so much mischief at boarding school, I waited outside all night on a chair until the shop opened. She was ahead of me and bought a whole lot of clothes for her sisters and mother. You were allowed in one person at a time, and when it was my turn all that was left was a wedding dress! That shop wasn't really to my taste either, but it was fun to spend the whole night sitting there, people-watching. A white wedding dress with huge puffed sleeves and flounces, a real dress for a princess, a real dress in which to join the prince on his white horse. I could buy it for 150 guilders, reduced from 2,000. 'Just' purchased and hung in my wardrobe, for….? I wore it once to accompany Bert wearing his tennis garb to go shopping in the local supermarket – me sitting in the shopping trolley! How we laughed at the faces of the respectable locals. In the past two years I've seen Bert twice. He lives near my sister. He and I enjoy talking about those days.

Antonia from boarding school days now lived in my house, on the garden side. It took ages before she came to live there, and she didn't stay long, in my perception. The room had to be perfect before she moved in. I was gradually filling out if I look at how I was in photos taken then. I hadn't menstruated for a long time. I did still weigh myself every day and was aware of what I did and didn't eat. My hair had grown long again, hanging down to my bra fastener. It was lovely shiny hair. I suspect that, apart from my easy relationship with Bert, I was totally unaware of my womanhood. No feelings of arousal, of being desirable, longing. I wasn't familiar with such feelings any more. I never had or developed them during adolescence. I'd rejected them after having extinguished and denied my femininity at boarding school. I felt nothing and didn't know what I was supposed to feel or could feel. Bert naked – I saw his penis yet didn't see it. I looked, but unconsciously, unaware. I looked without really looking, in the way of so many people. I didn't see what was real about me or about other people I would meet.

I spent many school holidays with Antonia, my friend who was expelled from boarding school, and we turned them into great adventures. We're still bosom friends. Antonia lives on her own and has an antique shop in The Hague. Our past and our holidays have forged strong bonds between us.

We always hitchhiked. My father knew, and I told my mother we were going by train. I saved a thousand guilders for a four-week trip, combining my studies with Saturday and vacation work. I had an allowance of 500 guilders from which I spent 250 on rent, and my phone bills, food, clothes, and so on from the remainder. I saved a bit, not much – I found it hard to save, still do! Our first trip. We were planning to go to Spain but were given a lift to northern Italy by an Italian truck driver, Celestino. He had bright blue eyes. We were flexible. It was a stroke of luck to get a lift like that. And we didn't know Italy then. Antonia and I sat chummily in the cabin. We ate in a truckers' café, paying for our own food. As night fell, we had a problem. There were three of us: who would sleep where? I ended up beside the driver because Antonia said: "He'd rather have you next to him than me". At some stage he started pawing me, and with my motto of pretending not to notice, I allowed it. I acted as if I wasn't there, the way I'd learned to do at boarding school during my mental 'maiming' by the nuns. I don't know what he actually got up to. I do know that he began to feel me up in places my hands and fingers hadn't visited for years. I liked it, enjoyed it a great deal.

But I didn't do anything back, really didn't know how. Then he suddenly jumped up furiously and started cursing in Italian. That had never happened to him before. It makes me chuckle now, but at the time I was in a state of shock. I didn't know what was wrong and Antonia only said: "He's annoyed because you aren't doing anything". So, the engine was started up and away we went…I don't remember where. We called on his mother, to whom he complained his manhood had been damaged. Then on to the factory where he had to unload and load, and on to Bologna. By then he had realised I was as green as grass and we parted harmoniously. Antonia recently showed me a photo of a man with his arm round my shoulder. It turned out he had four fingers… I said to myself "just act as if you haven't noticed that arm round your shoulder". I'm having a bit of a giggle now, but it's more like weeping. How alienated can you become from yourself, how far can you stray from your true self at your very source. I, that child who originally approached the word so happily, with such abandon. Said exactly what she felt, both emotionally and physically…She had gone, locked away and the key had been lost. Seemingly that's how I then acted and managed to portray just that: the surface.

The following year, another trip to Italy and from there on to Yugoslavia – that was the plan. We got a lift, then walked a little way, already having crossed the border with Yugoslavia without realising it. We were picked up by two Italians, Aldo and Neri, who pointed out that we'd made a big mistake by crossing the border without the appropriate stamps. Back to Italy. We all got on well and decided to spend another two days together. Antonia and I always paid our own way on principle, also to avoid any difficulties – I wasn't that naïve! That night Antonia and I were in bed and I've no idea why we hadn't locked the door. Neri crept in and sat on the edge of my bed. His hands wandered under the blankets to my warm, private spot. I was somewhat stupefied, Antonia next to me and Neri on the edge of the bed. I didn't know how to react, pretended at first, I was asleep, had to wake up in the process. I pushed his hand away, no doubt saying something like "no, Antonia's here". I'm don't suppose I said I didn't want it… didn't dare. How awful: not daring to say you don't want something, something that isn't right at that moment, something you don't feel. Scared of not being liked. He was a nice man, but that's all. He left – another man whose manhood I'd injured. This time our relationship was intact. I acted as if nothing had happened. I did tell Antonia, she hadn't noticed a thing. We went with them to Trieste, we had lots of fun together, the four of us. Antonia and I had taken a hotel for one night and then hitchhiked further to Dubrovnik. We'd promised to visit it on the way back. All went well, hitchhiking. We got a lift from a lawyer, a man of around thirty who lived with his mother. She invited us to spend the night at her house. I don't remember the man's name, hardworking, kind to his mother and in love with me. He even proposed to me during those two days. And he didn't lay a finger on me! I thought the world was a funny old place. He was clearly upset when I said (I think) with a laugh: "Of course I won't marry you. You don't know me, and this isn't my world." Antonia and I continued our travels. It became more difficult to get a lift, short distances only. At some stage we got a lift from two men in a car with a trailer. It contained birds to be sold at the market in Dubrovnik. The men were rather grubby, dishevelled, market traders from a village. We had a set rule: get in the car together and always keep our rucksacks on our laps. If we wanted to get out, we could do so quickly. At some point we were driving on the coast road to Dubrovnik. A narrow road with a ravine on the ocean side – I was sitting on the ravine side. The co-driver took a bottle of slivovitz and began drinking and passed it to the driver. It was empty in no time, and the co-driver tried to grab my breasts under my sweater, pushing my rucksack to one side. He said, "Let's make sex" and grinned an almost toothless grin. I had just one thought: either the ravine or the fellow all over me. In a flash I opted for the latter. Just pretend it isn't happening. Antonia had a stiletto in her rucksack and tried to get it. The man grinned, opened the car's glove compartment and produced a gun. OMG! I'd started to push his hands away and then the driver began pawing Antonia. The car started to lurch backwards and forwards... A car behind us saw what was happening and overtook our car, blocking it. Apparently, they were acquaintances. We were able to get out of the car, shattered. Our femininity had been attacked, we'd faced death momentarily: death on the coast road. We were shivering like children who've got out of the bath and are cold...

We were crushed. We had to go on and there was no public transport where we were. We got a lift in another car and didn't report the offence. Who would believe us – and we were frightened too. We never hitchhiked again in Yugoslavia. Dubrovnik was a lovely city, still is. We planned to stay there for around four days, one to recuperate, two to see the sights and then back to Trieste by public transport, bus, train, and that would take at least two days. There were already a lot of tourists. Tourists have a guide – and that's how we got to know one called Milan. I thought Milan was marvellous, he was a student, spoke fluent English and he was good for a laugh. Plus, he was attractive: tall, well-built, merry eyes and a merry laugh. We liked each other, I was even turned on and that was really scary. Antonia noticed and said: "Sleep with him, it's good for you". He'd already asked me, and Antonia knew. It was hard, all the things that could happen. Also, my motto was – and is – "we're in it together". Antonia insisted, and I went ahead. I told him: "I'll sleep in your bed, but you mustn't do anything!" And he didn't. We just lay in each other's arms and kissed. I felt arousal in my private parts and that feeling terrified me. I couldn't accept it. The next day he left with his group. We left for Trieste. On arrival I regretted having refused – here was a man with whom I would have dared to do 'it'! By then I was 21 years old. Yes, I really regretted that decision.

Antonia insisted I return, just travel back. She would wait for me and then we'd have to go back to the Netherlands. I had five or six days. After day four she'd check at the station every day, there was one train a day. The journey would cost about 200 dollars. I had traveller's cheques. A lot of money! It was something I wanted to do and it was special of Antonia to encourage me. Fortunately, she had Aldo and Neri, and they were having a good time. They planned to go with us the Holland, to The Hague where we were living then. The journey was ghastly, all on my own. A long train journey, then a transfer to a bus, and another bus. I think altogether it was 15 to 20 hours, travelling through the day and night. I arrived at the hotel where Milan stayed when he was accompanying a group. There he was – and pleased to see me. As well as being surprised: he hadn't expected me. He managed to smuggle me into the hotel. I undressed shyly, stood there, completely naked. All he did was place me on the bed and penetrate me. It was finished before I knew, it hurt a lot, I didn't know what was going on and saw blood on the sheets. I was amazed. The sheets covered in blood, impossible, I had to rinse them, and he still had a appointment with his guests that evening. The room was on the first floor and I had to leave through the window. He first, and he would catch me. He missed! A piercing pain in my big toe. I was too offended to let on, not for all the tea in China. I said goodbye and went to a park, racked with pain. Sitting on a bench, licking my wounds. There were no mobile phones in those days and I felt horribly alone and unappreciated. The next day I returned, by bus, another bus, the train – and there was Antonia, waiting for me. I can't really remember. I was very pleased to see her. I think I told her that I'd acted tough, jumped out of the window. It was a good story. I didn't speak about my pain. I didn't know whether to laugh or to cry.

It transpired that I had broken my big toe. The bone was out of place and deformed. I had an operation and spent a week in hospital with 'that toe'. Until a while ago I would sometimes tell the story proudly – proud that I'd been prepared to spend so much time and money to be deflowered by the man I 'really' liked. That experience took me even further back than square one. I had dared to feel something and actually only felt pain, emotionally and physically. And I feel it again, tears pouring down my cheeks. I'm certain that many women reading this and thinking of their own situation will be crying with me…

Why do men abuse us and why do we let them abuse us!

Back in the Netherlands. Back to my studies, but first to the doctor – Dr. Van Breukelen – who was unable to suggest anything for my anorexia other than "pay no attention, it'll pass". I was scared I might be pregnant after the deflowering. Nothing wrong. I met Sjaak in a pub. We liked each other. I soon realised he didn't have a strong personality, a real old woman, often sickly, often out of sorts, and also a bit common despite coming from chic Wassenaar. He used crude terms for morning and evening erections. I was soon cured and broke with him. He couldn't take it and got friendly with Bert (who lived next door to me) so he could be close to me. I couldn't forbid it, but Bert and I had fewer 'board meetings'.

I went on to the next class – my final year at NXX. I did have my favourite subjects and lecturers: Maaike Meijer for Dutch. She was different – young, feminist, inspiring. Small in stature but large in her thoughts and actions. Gijs was the psychology lecturer. His lessons were difficult, and therefore so interesting. Other than that, much of the course was simple. On Fridays I always took a bag full of empty wine bottles to school. After school I passed by a wine-shop to have the bottles filled. One-time Gijs was teaching in a neighbouring classroom and I suddenly decided it would be nice if he came for dinner that evening. I went into the classroom and invited him – to which he said 'Yes". I quickly drew a little map of how to get there. Bought the upmarket NRC newspaper and a bottle of whisky (by then I knew what men found interesting and liked to drink).

Gijs came, it was a lovely evening spent with my lecturer. He had to make a phone call because he'd missed his train. "To see if someone can feed the cat." 'Someone' proved to be his girlfriend, Jet. Gijs spent the night – just sleeping, very enjoyable and safe. The next day he went sailing with his brother and I lent him a sweater. When I saw him on the Monday, he said: "Your sweater is on the coat-rack in the staffroom". I was astonished – the staffroom wasn't my territory. There I found a bag containing my sweater and a bottle of whisky, plus a note, saying: "With thanks, and to replenish the depleted drinks supply". A new bottle to replenish two glasses! I was confused. I didn't really know how to deal with it – I'd only invited him for a meal. We were only four years apart in age and I just liked him. I had no ulterior motive. A few days later Gijs invited me to go with him to a party for the drawing teacher, Leo. He wanted me to accompany him: "I think you're nice and fun!" Wow! That got me even more confused. My teacher taking me to another teacher's place. I went, and another teacher was there too. Gijs told me that he'd been in a relationship until recently. He'd broken with Jet, his girlfriend. They hadn't been getting on for a while and now the time was ripe. I wasn't pleased. I felt guilty. I hadn't invited Gijs in order to get him away from his girlfriend. He maintained I didn't need to feel guilty. The relationship would have ended anyway. I thought to myself: "That's something you hear often enough!"

Deep down I continued to feel bad about it. I felt the sadness I'd experienced when my cousin Christa took Alex away from me while I was at boarding school and she – and Alex – had free rein. So sneaky! Gijs prepared the exams at my house. I never saw any of the questions and in no way did I get preferential treatment.

In the end, Gijs was out of my league. I can now appreciate the prevailing attitude that such relationships are not a good idea – there is difference in status and so in power, and it is easy to abuse it unwittingly. I was the one who placed Gijs on a pedestal and considered myself to be very lowly! Thanks to him I started appreciating food. He liked/likes to cook and eat well. Italian cuisine was our favourite. I put on weight and started imitating Gijs a bit: his preference in music, his enjoyment of reading, his enjoyment of – you name it. I wanted to be clever and not that dull-witted NXX girl. Leading up to my NXX diploma I had a lot of traineeships. For various reasons, including my boarding school background, the relationship with my parents, and being an emotionally neglected child, I wanted to study pedagogics. Near Gijs, in Amsterdam, far from my parents.

I was happy to discover I could study in Amsterdam, yet nothing altered my feeling of loneliness, insecurity, fear. Deep down I always felt "It's my fault if the other person is sad or unhappy. It's due to me!" My self-image was lamentably low and if I dared to look at myself in the mirror, I saw a supremely sorrowful, insecure woman, whom I could no longer handle.

My life had become unbearable…

3 years old. Sorong New Guinea.

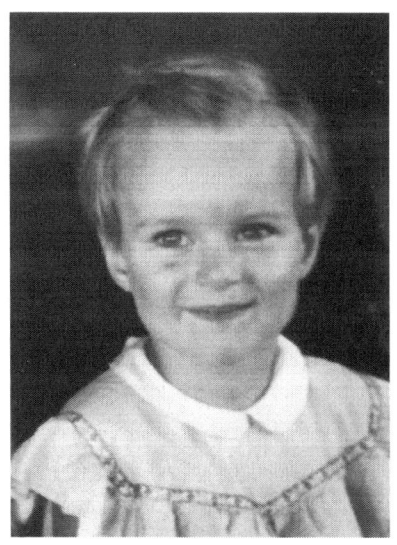

3 years old. Sorong, New Guinea.

Family portrait, 5 years old. During leave in The Netherlands.

Our house in Africa, Nigeria, Port Harcourt 1959

12 years old. Choir in Monster. (me far right at the back)

15 years old. Christmas celebration at boarding school, I am reading aloud a Christmas story.

17 years old. School camp in France. 4th grade Havo.

Grandma Graaf.

28 years old. On the sailing boat with Frans.

*46 years old. Oudezijds Voorburgwal, Amsterdam.
Picture taken by Roel.*

*47 years old. Oudezijds Voorburgwal, Amsterdam.
Picture taken by Arno Beers.*

*Mother and daughter (83 and 51 years old).
Picture taken by my father.*

At the crossroads

So, I went to Amsterdam, with my lamentably low self-image. Amsterdam, the city where everything was to change for me – or so I hoped. In fact, it was the same hope I had when I was sent to boarding school that everything would change when I was back home for the weekends. As if a fairy godmother had strewn stars before my eyes.

I had two problems, one being money. I didn't have a grant as my father was earning enough to pay for me. I could get an interest-free loan of 2,000 guilders from the State. And the tuition fees were 1,000 guilders. I secured the loan but had to pay the remainder myself. Rent, travel expenses, clothing, food, drink, books, everything! My father – because he decided everything – considered one course sufficient. I didn't!

Pedagogics – I wanted to help parents and children to lead a more loving life and keep it that way. I have driven: if I really, passionately want something, I'll go all out for it, whatever the consequences. Then no mountain is too high. That's still what keeps me happy. How to solve the money problem? I wanted some easy earnings. I applied at a model agency in Amsterdam – they existed back then too! I was fairly attractive again, almost the right measurements, though I made one condition: no lingerie shows! Back home in The Hague I started to have my doubts. I didn't want to earn money with my body, and I phoned to call it off. Looking back, I think I was still having problems with my body. As a model you have to be self-assured and I was anything but. I was also convinced that to earn a lot you had to exert yourself. Probably a conviction picked up at home: blood, sweat and tears – you had to undergo them!

I became a train stewardess. That was hard work! Two days on and two days off. Starting at 6 a.m. and often not home before 10.30 p.m. It was particularly gruelling, physically. You had to stock up with crates of food and drink yourself, make coffee and tea, push a swaying cart through the train. As well as serving in the restaurant car: killing. It was impossible to combine a daytime job and a daytime study course. In those days they didn't have evening or part-time courses combined with a few days working on the train. And I continued with the train job in the vacations.

The other problem that could be termed 'interesting' was a special entrance exam I had to take because I had to study statistics. It was very difficult, but I passed, and very proud this time. Not everyone was successful. And there was a third problem – somewhere to live! I moved in with Gijs, temporarily. He had a room, measuring 20 squares metres. It had patio doors leading into a communal garden. The kitchen and bathroom were shared with four other people. Gijs had a bed-settee. I loved being there with him. During the day I was working or attending lectures, and, in the evening, we were together. Yet I wasn't happy. I was scared of losing Gijs, unsure of how

I looked, of who I was. At all events, not good enough for anything. At night I often lay awake in bed. Gijs' desk was beside the bed and the cupboard on my side contained booze. He had some delicious grappa's – four different kinds. To ensure it wasn't too noticeable I took a different bottle each evening, pushing them around so you couldn't see that one was getting emptier than the other. I drank two glasses, just knocked them back, and then conked out. Gijs also had Dutch gin, and I liked that too.

I also earned money cleaning for Betty. I'd seen an advertisement for a cleaner and reacted. That Betty didn't want me: I was a student and students can't clean. I said on the phone – ringing from a phone booth since you didn't have your own phone in those days – "At least you could give me a trial, then I can prove I'm very good at cleaning!" She liked that. Betty and I became friends and did quite a lot of joint study projects. For instance, a 'drop-in' project for inmates of a women's prison, acting as contacts with the outside world. In that way we gave the inmates appropriate guidance and furthered their contacts with one another. During the summer, when no-one was there to protest, the prison managed to put a stop to the project, the excuse being it was too dangerous for us. We were dangerous for the management! The women's demands kept on growing!

I could take a bath at Betty's after work, and we started with breakfast – after which I worked very hard! Betty is still a friend, and I keep in touch with her son, daughter and their 'kin'. I go to all their family parties, and vice versa. I'm their family friend. That's how things can pan out.

I wasn't well off. Betty recommended her family doctor to me – doctor Van Woud. At my first appointment I explained my financial circumstances to him. He told me he had some patients to whom he didn't send a bill. That sounded kind!

Gijs' accommodation was too small, and anyhow he didn't want to share. I found rooms in Amsterdam. The rent I paid there – 450 guilders for two small attic rooms with no heating, no kitchen, no toilet – was almost as much as that of the principal tenant. Incredible! But there was no alternative. Even back in those days it was hopeless to find accommodation. The rooms were painted throughout: white for the sitting room and pale 'sky' blue for the bedroom. I bought a chemical toilet and cooked in the hall on a calor gas stove. In my sitting room I had an oil-fired stove, for which I had to lug jerrycans up 4 flights of stairs! I wasn't allowed to heat the bedroom – and it was freezing in the winter.It was hardship!

My studies were an uphill battle, too little time. There were more older students who, like me, had jobs. We joined forces, calling ourselves 'the evening group'. We made a lecture timetable and got together one evening a week. Discussing, swapping lecture notes. It was always special, companionable and stimulating. We had practical experience and that gave us a head start. The lecturers helped out, and even Gijs gave us practical's at Amsterdam University (for free), at my request. He was also working at Utrecht University as a psychology lecturer. At home in The Hague I had a neighbour with whom I had nothing in common. I did have friends, but all were dating someone, many were living as couples. Gijs and I met up mainly at the weekends. One Sunday evening, when Gijs was cooking our meal he suggested going to his parents in Alkmaar the following weekend. We did that often and stayed the night there. Suddenly, before we went to bed, he said: "I want to end our relationship". I didn't know what to say – I think I said: "But while you were cooking you suggested going to your parents!" "Yes, but I've been thinking about it for some time now." My whole world collapsed, I was winded, couldn't think straight, couldn't escape. All I could do was open the drinks cupboard and knock back a couple of drinks. I softly cried myself to sleep. I'm crying again now. It was so hurtful, and I'm back there, beside that bed, beside that cupboard, a distraught young woman, with a man sleeping deeply beside her. Lonely in her pain and distress.

We'd been together for a year and a half. It took me six years to let go of him completely.

I awoke the next morning, stunned. Gijs got up and went to Utrecht, to the university. Imagine it, he a psychology lecturer and then breaking off with his loved one at bedtime. What's the point of knowing how to act when you don't put it into practice. You shouldn't break bad news to someone, even on a Friday afternoon! Of course, emotions are emotions. But if you've been feeling a certain way for a while, wait for a more fitting moment. I'm a nice person, I'm never really angry or resentful – whatever happens to me, my love usually conquers my ego. Not right away. I too want to be liked. In situations like that I'm just 'gentle Sylvia'.

I remember it well: I'd promised Gijs to alter the fur collar on his coat, the buttonholes were too big. I made them smaller before I left, before cycling home I bought a rose and left it on his desk. That's all. I was torn apart. As I write, I'm experiencing it all over again. Gijs was the love of my life in those days. I felt comfortable with him, sexually, felt at ease with what I knew and enjoyed. I'd never had an orgasm, didn't know what it was, nor was it relevant at the time. I saw Gijs again that week and asked if he could tell me why it was off. He couldn't. He'd think about it and perhaps change his mind! Hope returned, longing, perhaps it would work out. It never did. The evening we'd arranged to see each other I saw Gijs walking along with a bag filled with my things, it contained a five-page letter. A letter full of psychology terms that ended with the words his "feelings towards me no longer warranted a relationship". I asked Gijs if he wanted to stay the night. I wanted to make love to him, feel him inside me, united deeply for the last time!

He protested, he didn't want to add to my pain. But what can a man do when a woman wants it. We made glorious love and the relationship was still off. Gijs had always thought I was alluring and attractive. We made love again, also I helped him move to a new house. While Gijs and I were still together when I went to an exhibition with Leo, our drawing teacher at school. He made wonderful paintings, Gijs already owned one. The paintings cost 600 guilders and I bought one, paying for it in instalments. Once I'd paid it off and the painting was actually mine, I still gave it to Gijs even though we were no longer an item. I'd bought it for him. I also gave him an authorised version of the Bible from Museum

Boijmans Van Beuningen. It was mine and he thought it was splendid. I intend to ask him to leave it to my children as he has none of his own.

At Gijs' thesis defence formalities, Jet (his girlfriend at the time he met me) and I were his only 'exes' to be invited. His current wife was there too. It was the first time Jet and I met. After 33 years she said: "I've got a very pressing question to ask you. That evening when you first came to Amsterdam with Gijs, did you sleep in my bed?" I could look her straight in the eye and say: "I lay on a mattress with Gijs on the floor at Hans' place". She gave me a grateful look.

After Gijs left me I went into a decline. I had to work hard. My self-image had received another blow and I had more problems sleeping. No-one apart from my friends, fellow students Joke and Agnes, noticed. I wanted to put on a brave face. The situation festered: "Not nice, interesting and alluring enough for a relationship". I could talk to Betty about it. One evening I was cycling home from some enjoyable event, was in a good mood and who should I almost knock over? Doctor Van Woud.

Sylvia: "Hey, doctor Van Woud", and gave him a look. He: "Nowadays I live across the road, I'm divorced. Do you feel like a drink?"

Wow, my family doctor inviting me for a drink!I went along, sitting agreeably on the sofa drinking whisky, something I rarely drank. Usually I only drank in order to sleep. After a few glasses, he had to leave to attend a birth. And I thought "OMG, after having drunk so much!" When I put it into words, he replied: "I'm hardened, and I can handle it!" He returned quickly and began kissing me passionately, pulling off my bra, dragging off my clothes – I'd learned from films and books that this was passion!

My doctor and me! Another night on a bed-settee, and when the alarm went off he had to rush to his surgery. I could take it easy. Between patients he came back to give me a kiss, caress me. Then it was time to go to my own home. I'd left a note with the phone number of the girl who lived next door to me, so he could ring and arrange for us to see each other. Often, I knocked at her door to ask if a certain doctor Van Woud had rung for me. After a couple of weeks, I went to his surgery. "Great to see you again. I've been busy, and I'll ring you for sure." It was almost my birthday and a dreamed of breakfast in the man's bed. I found a crumpled note in my letter box: on New Year's Eve he'd fallen in love with a damp-eyed woman and I could appreciate that breakfast in bed wasn't fitting. To add insult to injury, I got a bill for my visit to his surgery when I asked why I hadn't heard from him. I found a different doctor! And worst of all, this doctor knew of my grief at losing Gijs and my poor self-image, as well as knowing I'd had anorexia. I was of course part of it, yet I felt so used and misused – another doctor abusing his position! I've come across Van Woud now and then, as my own doctor's locum. Again, has he tried to seduce me with his charms and I did once think: "So what, I'll take him as a lover!"

I went to his house, taking a bottle of wine. Unbelievable, but true. An attractive woman came towards me, also carrying a bottle of wine. She stopped at Van Woud's front door. I was saved by the bell! It ended up badly for that doctor. He made mistakes, was hospitalised for his drinking problem and finally ended his life by means of alcohol and pills. Betty told me that.

Meanwhile I was obliged to work even harder to earn money. I got the job of dental 'assistant'– for the uncle of Wilma, the new girl next door. The dentist was a widower. I breakfasted at his house twice week, answered the phone, made appointments and served as a sounding board. I was also working for Betty and living on the poverty line. The dentist was odd. He liked to give me sherry and then get me to clean the parquet floor with the polisher – and watch me. Someone watching me yet again, like the medical director at Bethel Hospital and the gym teacher at primary school. I didn't want the sherry, but he insisted and won – it was so jolly, and he was going through such a bad patch. Sylvia pleasing someone again…

I think I worked for him for around a year. There was a time when, again, I'd had a few sherries and he hung some of his deceased wife's jewellery round my neck. I'd talked to my good friend Wilma about her uncle and she agreed that she'd also had an odd proposition from him. Anyway, the jewellery round my neck and his look, ugh…, I said: "I don't want this, I'm not a whore!" He slapped me hard on my cheek. I packed my bag, never to return. Until about five years ago that man rang me every year on my birthday to wish me many happy returns. He also said: "After my wife's death you were the one who took good care of me, you were more to me than my children". I moved houses a lot, but he still managed to track me down. By now he must be well into his nineties if he's still alive. Wilma understood my reaction.

I had a dart board in my white attic room. One of Wilma's and my 'entertainments' was to drink gin-and-tonic and throw the darts through the room at the chosen spot, like a couple of 'wild women'. Great fun, and as sick as dogs the next morning. Wilma's solution was to buy two cakes at the bakers at the corner, making us even more wretched and throwing up afterwards. Wilma moved to Leeuwarden. She married Oeds, with whom she already had a relationship. She has two sons, the same age as my daughters: now 28 and 25. We kept in touch until the children were around 18, phoning each other and getting together on important occasions. I must ring her again.

No job, less money. Yvonne, whom I met during my traineeship at the children's home and who is still a friend, was my other friend for a weekend night out. We shopped together at the market on Saturdays, after which I would take a shower at her place. Taking a bath at Betty's and a shower at Yvonne's – I didn't need to visit the bathhouse. Dinner at Yvonne's and then out on the town. I spent the night at her house if I hadn't given up in the meantime. The only photo on her bedside table was of me, and she's not a lesbian! I can't remember if Yvonne stopped as well. To some extent that's the way things were those days. Also, and primarily, it was my lack of self-respect and sex – of which my idea was distorted. It was normal to go home with someone after a good night out. It wasn't such a big deal. I still hadn't reached an orgasm, nor was I very imaginative – I just let it happen. And if I wasn't enjoying it, I used my 'trick' – pretend you don't feel a thing!

I remember that I left a pub and went with someone my age to his place. While I was undressing and looked at the guy, I thought: "What am I doing here". I told him: "This is a mistake, I'm going home!" I know how proud I was, I'd crossed a line and said I didn't want something! I rarely dared to. Nowadays I think: go ahead and offend! If you do something you don't want or feel, and so cross your own line and that of the other person. But… I wanted to be liked as well!

I was so scared of not being liked and didn't really know how to handle sex. By then it wasn't related love. It was related to my old traumas.

Not being liked, being abandoned because you're not worthy, being to blame if the other party doesn't feel comfortable. Hell up!

Meanwhile I'd seen an advertisement. A vocational school in Rotterdam was looking for someone to teach crafts and child care, at the lowest level with the most difficult students. The current teacher was going on maternity leave. With my financial worries, I decided to apply, and was invited for an interview. I had a terrible hangover on the day. I don't know how the interview went. I'd told Betty and she said; "Go, if only for the experience of applying for the job – you've never done it before."

I went, was very relaxed, had strong views on teaching, and my love of children was abundantly clear. Also, my affinity with very difficult children. Mrs. Groen, the school head, rang me at Betty's: they'd chosen me, despite my lack of experience. They had confidence in me and the teacher I was to substitute for sensed my love for young people.

Amazing! I got that job. I'd accepted, not realising how hard it would be. I had to travel from Amsterdam to Rotterdam three times a week It meant leaving home at

5.50 a.m. three times a week, to be in Rotterdam to start teaching at 8.30 a.m. My own studies were hard-going, also because I had to do a daytime course partly in the evenings. And now I had to prepare, and check course work for my students in the evenings. Everything was new, and I wasn't particularly proficient. I was very fond of my students, and they of me. I was popular, I understood them, taught with my head, heart and soul and was interested in their home situation, their thoughts about who they were, how they felt – in fact, more of a teaching mentor. As far as my own studies were concerned, I had no time for college life. I was always either working or studying. It was really hard-going and lonely. At a party I met Frans, he was an internist. He liked me, his wife was a fellow student of mine. He asked for my phone number and I told him: "Ask your wife, she's got it". In the end I said: "I'll tell you just once!" By then I had a landline phone. It was required for my job in Rotterdam for which I had to be reachable by phone and could also phone the school easily myself. One day the phone rang, and it was Frans. We went for lunch at Keizer, a stylish 'bodega' in Amsterdam – I did feel chic! We had salmon and white wine, and a well-known Dutch television actor and comedian was having lunch at the next table. I felt rich and a real woman! I wore a nice dress, high heels – it was like a dream. His wife knew. Correct. I'd told her about it and we agreed if she was uncomfortable with the situation, I'd side with her and drop Frans.In fact, he played an important part in my life for a long time. He thought it was good for me to have a real partner instead of my boyfriends. If I did have a boyfriend, it didn't mean the end of Frans. When

I entered into a real relationship and set up house with the man in question, my friendship with Frans became one without sex – which was difficult for him. I saw him again not long ago, after ten years of silence.

I was in love with him for a while, though I knew he would never leave his wife for me – or anyone. Things were extra complicated as a result. At school, the teacher's maternity leave was over. I was offered a job working two-and-a-half days a week, they didn't want to lose me. And I accepted. I really enjoyed being with my pupils and the teaching side, apart from all the preparation – that was horrible. I had few parallel classes, meaning there was a great deal of preparation and marking. One time I asked Agnes, my friend who had also been at the NXX, to help me with the marking. It was just too much, marking work night after night. You didn't have a mobile phone in those days. I worked at a branch of the school on Thursdays and Frans sometimes rang me there to make a date. He would be waiting at the station after a hard day's work and would take me out to dinner. That was great. Getting off the train, falling into your loved one's arms, both of you so happy, the batteries recharging. But sometimes it was tough. I couldn't see Frans when I longed to, he had a wife and child/children from a former marriage, and his hospital and his friends. Mrs. Groen, who was very fond of me, took good care of her staff. She summoned me one day and asked: "Is everything all right?" She was more sympathetic and concerned than my own mother. She knew of my relationship with Frans, my studies and all the exams I had to pass to get my bachelor's. One day she said: "Stay home tomorrow, you need a day off, we'll organise things here". I hadn't asked for anything, she'd just observed and sensed it. She was very much ahead of her times. The mood at school was especially nice on Fridays, in the lunch break. The ladies drank sherry together, we took it in turns to bring a bottle, and the men went to the pub. I went with them! Always beer with a chaser. I got on well with my male colleagues, I still enjoy male company. Their humour, not 'yes, but.', men are up front.Later one of my male colleagues told me: "I always liked you but was afraid I'd never have you to myself". All that happened at Mrs. Groen's school. A lot happened – enough to fill an entire book!

The course was hard going, particularly Statistics. Peter, a fellow student and a good friend, gave me some coaching. He was a dear. He was very fond of me (we're now both on LinkedIn) and I of him, though we weren't into anything physical. I had various male friends, and invariably the nicer I thought they were, the less they turned me on. A couple of friendships broke up as a result. At the time I didn't understand, I do now! My relationship with Frans caused a great deal of unrest in my life. Never sure when I'd be seeing him. Working hard, the tough studies – life for me was hard, very hard. Cold in my attic room and too little time for socialising. I was lonely. I can't remember my parents ever having visited me in my attic. My sister had her life in Leiden and later back in The Hague. I went on holiday a few times with her, sometimes we were close and then distant for a long time. Once we went to southern Italy, hitchhiking near the Côte d'Azur. A sports car with two handsome men stopped, we got in and were able to stay at a country villa belonging to one of them. It was large enough. When we arrived, there was a fire burning in the fireplace with a large white sheepskin in front. As if it was perfectly normal, I undressed and lay down naked on the rug – I'd once seen something like that in a film! Then I got dressed again. I could lose myself in my imaginary world and in my childishness, it was genuine. I didn't want more. But rather crazy, looking back, knowing what I do now. We had a drink and one of the men showed me round. He was called Antonio. He was fun and cheerful, and we ran through the house. I was shown one room after another, and each time he threw me on a bed. In the last room he pulled off my trousers and screwed me. Trousers back on! I do know I called them 'the Antonio trousers', they contained his sperm. I wore them during the rest of that day and the next. Who was I? What was normal?

I had more and more problems sleeping and drank at least three glasses of gin to get to sleep. In the train, I'd order a bottle of water or the like from a former colleague to clear my head on my way to school. I was overtired. In my private life too – my self-confidence dropped further and further due to my weariness. There was little evidence of my childhood pluck – I could hardly remember how to spell it! When I invited friends round for a meal I worried for days, could hardly decide what to cook and was uncertain about the result. Mrs. Groen noticed my weariness and gave me another day off. She sensed my unhappiness. My teaching didn't suffer demonstrably. One evening I was preparing a crafts lesson – a plaster mouth made in a mould – I was planning to make the mouth with the pupils. My experiment didn't work and in frustration I threw all the plaster down the sink in my self-made counter top. Result: all the pipes in the house were blocked. The plumber had to be called in. The first thing he said was: "Child, what a place!"

With his, and Frans' help I was able to move to a different place six months later: half of a house, where I could live for about five years until it was demolished. I felt I should stop with my work in Rotterdam. It couldn't go on like that. I'd completed my bachelor's course and chose to study Ortho pedagogics, or remedial education – behavioural and learning difficulties. I was familiar with that problem area. My teaching job did not tie in sufficiently with my studies and in the summer, I was supposed to do a traineeship, so I'd have to stop work anyway. I asked if I could have a talk with my father, and my sister was there too. My father valued her opinion. Also, it meant he didn't have to take sole responsibility. I told them how bad things were, something I often told them previously. My parents and sister knew about Frans. I never had secrets or a double agenda. I also told my father how stressed out I was and asked if he would help me. I'd repay him later. My father felt – and my sister agreed – that it would be irresponsible to give up a job. Such a good job. I should pull myself together and perhaps I could arrange something at my school for the traineeship, like an extra assignment tying in with my studies. Inconceivable. I'd had anorexia, had already suffered from chronic stress – and again my arguments fell on deaf ears.

One morning the alarm woke me, and I couldn't get out of bed. My body was leaden, I had difficulty breathing. I could no longer think. I rang school at 8.15 a.m.

and got Mrs. Groen on the line. I wept, telling her: "I can't go on, I'm done in, I don't know what to do, I'm so ill!" She replied: "Go back to bed, take time to get better, I'll arrange things here. Ring later in the week to let me know how you are". I was worse, not better. Today it would be described as an extreme burnout. Every week a letter arrived through my letterbox, not from my mother, but from Mrs. Groen. A letter telling me how my pupils were getting on, my colleagues, the current state of affairs, and in particular, expressing loving thoughts for me. The way a mother comforts her child, encouraging, trusting all would turn out fine. It didn't. I wanted to get better, I missed my pupils. Each week I found a bundle of letters and cards in the letterbox: "We miss you, Miss", "Miss, I don't know you, I'm a new pupil, but I've heard so much about you, get well soon, the new teacher isn't nice". The same pleas every week. There came a time that getting up became easier and I wanted to give it a go – just return to my school for an afternoon, see 'my pupils'. I managed, without feeling nauseous, to cross the schoolyard. "Miss, Miss" – I couldn't say a word, I think I wept. I told Mrs. Groen I wanted to hand in my resignation. I couldn't, didn't want to continue.

Deep down, I didn't want to go on, absolutely no longer. My old resilience and optimism had disappeared completely, I'd lost my way, lost myself. If I couldn't even help myself, how could I help others? My studies were pointless, everything was pointless… I wanted to die. Not from physical pain this time, like after my moped accident, but from emotional, mental pain, locked in my stressed-out body and mind. I went to my new family doctor, the one following the drama with Van Woud.

Told him of my death wish. I am crying, becoming for a moment that woman again. Life was so unbearable, I couldn't see a way out. I told the doctor I was an alcoholic, suffering from stress, uncertain and unable to cope with life. I was done in. I'm so glad I went to the doctor and didn't do away with myself in a fit of panic. I'd fantasised about it. He referred me to the Riagg (ambulatory mental health service). In the course of three years I relived my entire life, guided by Mrs. Leidsvrouw. Gradually my self-respect, self-love, womanhood, the normal, fundamental life skills returned or were developed. During the final session I asked if I might read my intake interview with the resident psychiatrist. It began: "An attractive young woman entered the room, and at every question I asked her she gave me an enquiring look as if she needed approval for her answer". When I'd finished reading, I said: "What a terribly difficult time that woman was having!" I was visibly emotional.

My relationships

The plunge was taken to find myself 'again'. But then the road proved to be very long. Just as the road to curing my anorexia had been. Though they were certainly the right decisions.

Mrs. Groen had blocked my resignation. I was allowed to stay home for almost six months, until the summer, to regain my strength. I got public assistance. Before the summer holidays I was given a big farewell party, as if I'd worked there all my life. Then they released me, with a heavy heart.

I see Mrs. Groen about once a year. She's in her nineties now. I ring her a couple of times a year and we send each other letters on our birthdays. She was a mother to me.

Frans was also very kind. He often turned up in the lunch break bringing delicious sandwiches, and of course he often wanted a cuddle too. I don't remember if that was what I wanted, I was worn out. My parents, my father in particular, were shocked. I don't think he ever realised how bad things were, he was emotionally constipated though easily inclined to be weepy. As you are with a tear-jerker song, for instance. With Frans' help I composed a letter to the Minister of Education, explaining my problems concerning my traineeship and my parents' unwillingness to help out financially. They received a reply, from the Minister addressing "the unwilling parents of Sylvia Duijm". My parents were furious and disappointed that I had done such a thing. However, my father did say he would finance me during the year of my traineeship, but not a day longer! I'd organised a trainee post at the Institute of Pedagogy and Psychology in Amsterdam, in the day shelter for dropouts! They were very pleased to have me. The post was for a year, four days a week plus one study day, as I recall. I had teaching experience with a troublesome target group, was somewhat older and my enthusiasm and ideas were unimpeachable. I didn't tell them about my burn-out.

Meanwhile I'd moved, to accommodation above a shoe shop, Van Haren. The shop owned the property and in those days the city council had the right to decide to whom the dwelling would be let – one time it was the owner, the other time the council. It was the city council's turn. Frans managed to break in, thanks to the upstairs neighbours. I paid the rent to Van Haren right away. My sister and her boyfriend helped me move my things and I went to live there. Gijs put down a new floor in the new house, and Dé, who was a friend and occasional lover (and single) built a bed in a recess. I didn't get any further than a corner of the room, trembling like a leaf, scared, insecure, weary. Moving to a new house when you have a burn-out is far too gruelling. And then my breasts were hurting. When Frans hugged me, I would say: "Ow!" It turned out that I had lumps in my breasts, admittedly benign, but they had to be removed. That was scheduled for the autumn half-term break in my traineeship. Again, something impacting my self-image and even more so, my womanhood. caused by the burn-out. Everything I'd gradually managed to build was lost. My new accommodation was pleasant. Larger and warmer, I had a proper toilet and shower in a tiny space. Also, a kitchen with French windows opening onto the extension of the shoe shop below. I actually had a roof terrace! Meanwhile Olaf, a friend of Yvonne's (where I used to take a shower) had fallen in love with me. He was kind, concerned, a little gloomy, and I didn't feel any 'chemistry' with him. He was crazy about me, showered me with presents. That year I went on holiday with my sister and Jeanette, a college friend. After all, I had a holiday allowance. Jeanette lived around the corner from my new place. She supported me in my miserable, exhausted period. We flew to Greece and took the boat to Lesbos. Two weeks. Jeanette was supposed to go for one week and then on to her Greek friend, Christos. At the time I had another problem. Despite my burn-out I looked good – I can see that from the photos taken then. But I wasn't aware of it. I'd always attracted men's attention, I was used to it. Sex or not, I got on well with them on the whole. Nice and up front!

We arrived in Greece, a brief visit to Athens and on to Lesbos. The harbour was full of men and women with rooms to let. I remarked, naively: "Oh how nice, they're making an effort, you don't even need to look for a place." We were taken by surprise and went along with a boy of our own age – his uncle let rooms. It was a disappointment. All I remember is that we slept in the sitting room and had to use their private bathroom. I've forgotten the rest. The uncle was very nice, the nephew too. Early the next morning we went fishing. I've got a photo of the uncle, probably about 40 years old, a weathered face.

I didn't sleep in a bed. Jeanette and my sister did, and I slept on a mattress on the floor. The nephew was staying there too, sleeping on the mattress behind me. I was tired, vulnerable and did my 'act as if you don't notice' trick again. Pretending to sleep, I let him 'f…' me, to put it coarsely. He lay behind me and, half-asleep, I just let it happen. He didn't make a sound and the others didn't notice anything. No condom, nothing. Denied it completely. And off fishing the following day!

We wanted to visit the other side of the island, it was really pretty there. Looked for a small hotel. I got a frightful itch in my vagina, and a discharge. The first time in my life there was an after-effect of my 'denial'. I saw the local doctor, ashamed of my imprudent behaviour. I had a venereal disease, not dramatic, but bad enough. I had to go back to the doctor after about five days. By then my sister and Jeanette knew. Jeanette went back to Athens, to Christos. My sister and I stayed behind. We went to the seaside, visited some little towns, our hotel was very simple, too simple. I became very ill and instead to going back to the doctor for a check-up, he had to come to me. I was vomiting a lot and had diarrhoea. The doctor was handsome, looked like Elvis Presley in his better days. I had a fever, almost 40 degrees Celsius, and it lasted at least two days. I had paratyphoid fever! 'Elvis' came twice a day and the hotel people took it in turns with my sister to check that I didn't lose consciousness. I was very ill. So, my sister did have some holiday. She'd met a soldier – a sergeant – in the hotel, a nice man who took her for walks and entertained her while I was delirious.

He was very kind to us both. My sister's boyfriend had alerted my parents and Olaf. He was working in Amsterdam and was living in my apartment, meaning he didn't need to travel. I had two cats, siblings, for him to take care of. Olaf lived around the corner, so he also knew. Remarkable. Olaf was a very nice person. He wanted to take a plane immediately, to visit me. I definitely didn't want him to. My feelings for him weren't exactly clear. I didn't want to burden him – or myself. I didn't want anything. I was so ill. Then it was time to go home. The insurance enabled me to get a first-class cabin. I was so nauseous – all I did was stand on deck, vomiting over the railing. At Schiphol airport my parents, Olaf and my sister's boyfriend were waiting for us.

In the plane home we discovered we were both dreading going back to our own homes and the lives we lived there. We were dreading the encounter. On arrival we all went out for a meal together in a splendid restaurant that Olaf had recommended. He had good, expensive tastes.

I recovered, and it was time for my traineeship. By then it was evident that my friendship with Olaf would never be a love affair. We didn't match, either in character or as people, I thought he was dull. He was mad about me and thought my energy and the 'Sylvia' that I was were wonderful! Unfortunately, I couldn't surrender myself to him. His body didn't arouse me in the least. I told him honestly what I felt, I thought I was being brave and sincere. I didn't want to offend Olaf. He was furious. A few days later there was a letter from him in my letterbox. I was the best thing that had ever happened to him. He found me so honest, sharing my real feelings with him, even if they were painful to him. He also wrote: "I've learned a lot from you, about honesty, passion and single-mindedness. Thank you for that" and he wished me the very best. I never saw him again. It was good to read it, though it changed nothing in my feelings of loneliness, insecurity and anxiety. I continued to feel it was my fault if the other party was sad or miserable. I was to blame. My self-image was lamentable and if I really looked at myself in the mirror, made contact with my soul, the look in my eyes, I still saw the supremely sorrowful, insecure woman, whom I could no longer handle.

Life was still unbearable!

I'd started therapy, but I had such a long way to go. I remember the first session. I had to wait a long time, too long to my mind. The therapist kept calling people in, a man then a woman, and so on. I actually felt too well to be sitting there, it was so stuffy. I wasn't allowed to smoke, and although I was supremely sorrowful, I considered the therapist to be aloof, it was no use. It got off to a difficult start, until I accepted that it that it would take its own course and we are all the way we are. Logical, but oh so difficult! I wanted it, but in my way. I still tend to be like that, though now I can smile and I'm better at letting go.

My traineeship began when I was in the middle of therapy. The students were the most damaged young people imaginable. Booted out by their parents and school. They'd lost their way, were completely lacking in self-esteem, no longer motivated and so lashing out, left, right and centre.No-one was any good but they themselves! It was the best school I've ever had in my life. And vice versa. I used to have – still do – a down-to-earth approach. Let's just get on with it, with my enthusiasm to boot. That's my approach, as a teacher and as an individual. The director, Paul, was amazed, as he put it: "You can even get the biggest s.o.b. to work!" He was referring to a time when I got punkers, skinheads and discos, the whole mob making paper flowers! Incredible, seriously. I'm familiar with such powerful enthusiasm, it just happens. Perhaps it also goes with a 'master of passion'.

Soon enough I discovered that the prevailing teaching method was inadequate for young people of that type. I was unable to go along with a *laissez-faire* policy for youngsters with little self-esteem, little or no motivation, and not knowing what they wanted. I had other ideas. What they needed were a tight programme, with fixed times for starting and ending, not too many options, strict observation criteria – all to promote a feeling of security. I wrote a policy paper and distributed it in a staff meeting. I linked termination of my traineeship with it, should they not agree with my approach! It worked. I was asked to apply for the job and was hired. Again, my father could quickly waive my payments. I was proud, very proud. The job was very hard work, 40 hours a week, alongside my therapy. And I still had a low self-image, just like the target group I was working with! I could empathise with them, those youngsters, sometimes too well, and I would be busy with them day and night. I worked there for 12 years and could write a book about that time. I was extremely fond of my pupils, I was warm, encouraging, allowed them to experience a lot about life, about themselves, taught them perseverance, and above all, I was consistent. A person should have a genuine need and not a fib toe get benefit payment, you should work on a realistic perspective, no alcohol or drugs in school hours. I dismissed a couple for messing about, telling them: "first end up in the gutter, you're still too well off". I've sometimes encountered former pupils, in the street or because they tracked me down through Google. Still grateful! I came across another former pupil (now herself a mother) with her daughter. She was 16 when she was in my class. When we met in the street, she told her daughter, with a proud look: "This is my teacher, Sylvia, she was the first person in my life who taught me how to learn". And she added: "I'm going to teach my daughter the same thing". I taught them how to learn in a wider context. My own thoughts at that moment were: "Come what may, I haven't lived for no nothing!"

My life still amounted to working hard, loving a lot, weary from work, as well as studying, because there was still a lot to be done for my studies. Again, job combined with studies, this time closer to home, but more taxing as regards the target group. I regularly held survival camps in the Ardennes. What a strain, a fight with myself for survival, both physically and mentally. Then my burn-out put in a sneaky appearance. Life continued to be tiring. It wasn't easy to be back home alone after a hard day's work, either. Mrs. Leidsvrouw, my therapist, always said: "You're by no means ready for a relationship yet, leave it a few years". At the time I didn't understand, now I do. I am fully aware that you must be able to love yourself unconditionally, warts and all, before you can build up a relationship with someone else. That is a necessary prerequisite. I've still tripped up a few times. I have hoped and thought that if someone loved me and I loved them everything would be all right, without realising exactly what it entailed. And accordingly, yet another married man crossed my path, a colleague this time: Laurence. Unhappily married, unable to talk to his wife about it, complaining to me and giving and taking 'love' when it was convenient in his relationship. The same old pain yet again, back to the waiting room, again easily pleased. The times with boyfriends continued, to a lesser extent admittedly, but it was wonderful to have attention, and all manner of thoughts go through your head: "When you're alone you're alone. I'm not hurting anyone. Perhaps it will work out…" By then I'd had breast surgery and gone back to work too soon, result: the scar is still a scar!

I got on well with Paul, the school's director, his wife Annette and their two small children, Roy and Marianne. We became close friends. I regularly babysat for them and was a family friend. Paul also thought highly of my expertise and I was a member of his policy group. I often accompanied him on visits to external contacts in order to learn the 'director's job'. The first summer I was working there I went on holiday on my own in my new 500-guilder car, a Simca, with my racing bike, a tent and my typewriter. I had to write a paper for my studies. I'd booked at a 'nature' camping site for 10 days, after which I'd join Annette and Paul in Groningen, where they had rented a house. I'd put my tent up there. I like my privacy! My parents were also planning to visit me at the camping site, as well as my colleague, Niels – also on his own like me. He was in love with me and I liked him. Niels was a true artist, he taught drawing and painting, was not at all typical.

My parents' visit was a disaster. They came to tell me, quite unemotionally, that they were separating: my mother would live in their vacated apartment in The Hague and my father would continue to live in Halsteren, a village in the province of North Brabant. That had originally been their second home, but latterly so attractive that it became their principal residence. It was for the best. My father would give my mother a good allowance, pay for her holidays, they would not get a divorce. My father was 'having it off' with Lotte, a mutual friend. My world collapsed, not because they were separating but the way they were going about it. After all the distress, me being to blame for their bad marriage, the 'reward' of boarding school and then this announcement, made in this way. We went for a walk and then they left. My mother was to live in The Hague and my father in Halsteren. Until her death, my mother kept reminding us that our father was a good man. Niels' visit wasn't a success either – I had to disappoint him about my feelings.

Lotte became a predicament. A couple of years later I helped my father to escape from Halsteren. Lotte was jealous, gave my father absolutely no latitude. She even locked him up on one occasion! He never returned to Halsteren. He lived for a year with my sister and her boyfriend, in their attic, before he could buy an apartment. It was hard going for them, even though my father wasn't difficult, he didn't make a nuisance of himself. They all dealt with it very well. The Halsteren house had to be sold. And after the year in my sister's attic, he pleaded with my mother to go back to him. He bought an apartment in The Hague and my mother did return – as she put it, because "she felt sorry for our father". They continued in the same old way. They were never able to take the step towards Love with a capital 'L'. While my parents were separated I had a very hard time. For a while, at least six months, I wouldn't see them. I was so angry, so…, all my emotions ran wild. The distance was a good thing, temporarily. I had to deal with everything that had happened in the chapters I have called 'Counting to ten' and 'Girlhood misery', and before I could resolve the distressing feeling that all my misery had been in vain. Now I know better: it was necessary so that I could become the person I am today, but it was grim. Now I'm happy with who I am, usually!

After those six months I regularly visited them. One weekend in The Hague, the next weekend for myself, then to Halsteren and the following weekend for myself. It meant I saw each of them once a month. I was very busy with my job and myself so that, apart from unusual occurrences, their lives rather passed me by. My mother had an affair with the son of one of the residents in the apartments. She was unable to abandon herself to him, perhaps concerned about her body, or perhaps too straitlaced, also his regional accent irritated her.

One Saturday I was in the train to Halsteren, reading the newspaper and, standard procedure, the personal ads (i.e. the 'lonely hearts column'). Not that I intended to react, just out of curiosity, although… This time there was an advertisement, at least a quarter of a page long, by someone called Paul. Wow, what an effort and a lot of money for an ad., and a really good one! I decided to react, a 'first' for me. My reply was very arrogant – just one sentence on the back of a photo: "The fact that I'm reacting should be enough!" A nice photo of me on Frans' yacht, toasting with a glass of white wine. And indeed, a few days later there was a reply. He wanted to meet me. We arranged at the Molenpad café in Amsterdam. The closer the day came, the less I felt like it. I actually wanted to call it off, but I'm also inclined to think in for a penny in for a pound. And I didn't want to offend the man at the last minute.

The Saturday in question arrived. It was nice weather. Wearing my tight pants, high heels and a khaki leather jacket, I cycled to the café. When I arrived, I propped the bike against a tree. Outside, three men were sitting in a row on a bench. All three looked nice! I sauntered past, so they could see me properly. One of them had seen my photo, but I hadn't seen one of him. Then I entered the café – no-one there. I sat down at a table and ordered a cappuccino from the barkeeper, he was called Jeroen. I waited, but no-one left the bench to come in. After about ten minutes I went back outside and asked the man in the middle (the nicest one) if he had written the ad. He looked at me in surprise and denied. Back inside. After a while the 'middle' man came up to me and said: "How amusing, you're here because of an advertisement? I don't want to intrude, don't want to queer your pitch, but I'd like to be the man in the ad." He left. After half an hour, having talked a bit to the barkeeper Jeroen and shared my frustration with him, I left. The next Monday there was a letter from the real Paul: he had been sitting on the left of the man in the middle and when I asked if he was the one, Paul had been so rattled that he had departed with his tail between his legs – could we perhaps plan another get-together? I'd had more than enough of the whole thing. Asked to have my photo back. Meanwhile I'd returned quite often to the café where I met the 'man in the middle' again. It was a brief affair. As usual, not enough guts, never any money and Sylvia having to cough up every time – as well as contracting a fine old fungal infection!

It took a while for me to realise what was going on, despite therapy. I still hadn't experienced 'true love'. Whenever I thought, this is it, it turned out to be a huge disappointment. Preceded by unrest, anxiety, waiting, despair, uncertainty about myself, then the self-esteem I'd built up faltered yet again. Still miserable.

I visited the café more often and got to know some people. I started at the fitness centre and then sometimes on to the Molenpad. It was always jolly. I hardly drank – I'd never been an alcoholic like I had stated at Riagg intake. In those days alcohol helped me sleep but didn't comfort me. For me it means conviviality, still. One day Jeroen the barkeeper said: "You make me so edgy. I like you and I'd like to take you out for a meal". And he did. Jeroen was a breath of fresh air. I was always working and studying, busy acquiring more and more knowledge and Jeroen was a simple barkeeper, with his outings and distractions. I didn't realise at the time that he was terrified of failure. That was the reason he was still a barkeeper. Jeroen was from Limburg (though he didn't have an accent), from a working-class family – the complete opposite of me. There, a middle school education was enough, for us it was derided.

He went south to celebrate carnival and I went skiing with Jeanette (the friend from the Greek 'adventure'). A student-type holiday like we'd had before, travelling by coach and staying in simple accommodation. I let Jeroen enjoy my Simca. On our return we had a meal in the restaurant where we'd been the first time. Jeroen told me that he'd had a 'threesome' with old friends – three of them having sex together, Two men and one woman. I couldn't believe my own ears. I was neither cross nor sad, my protection was to freeze – one of the three responses: fight, flight or freeze. I'd taught myself the latter. It kept going through my head, I just didn't understand: how could you do something like that, we were just becoming an item? And yet, perhaps I was being narrow-minded, perhaps you should be happy for the other person – it sounds like the stock phrase or even a book title: *As long as he's happy!* Jeroen explained it in such a way, it had 'just' happened, part of a loving friendship, that I accepted it rather than it is sounding alarm bells. Jeroen was oversexed, particularly mentally, to compensate for his insecure self-image.

Jeroen lived in a room on Keizersgracht canal. All he owned was an air gun and an eye pencil. He brought them with him when soon he moved in with me. He was cheerful, drove my Simca when he wasn't working – and he didn't work much, he was also receiving a state benefit. It was stopped when he came to live with me. I continued to work hard at the PPIA as well as studying. Jeroen provided light relief. He often picked me up after work and always had something original up his sleeve. We had plenty of fun together.

I'd always wanted children, preferably two daughters. I dreamt of having two emotionally stable girls who would contribute to collective consciousness! Women with more self-worth and self-respect, caring, loving and knowing what they really need, standing no nonsense for a bit of 'love and attention'. Women who love themselves.

Jeroen also badly wanted children, with me. We got married, for free on a Monday morning at 9 a.m. – merely because we wanted children. We didn't really need that marriage certificate. I proved to be 6 weeks pregnant. Before I actually became pregnant I had really given proper thought to the responsibilities of motherhood and momentarily wondered about it when I had my IUD removed… I wanted the device back! The gynaecologist refused.

A good friend and fellow student, Jonathan, did and didn't understand me. He was of Jewish descent and understood as no other the great responsibility. He also knew me very well and knew how I longed for children and loved them – as I had my entire life. I recall sitting with him on the university library steps. I felt his words liberated me: "'course you must persevere. It's something you've always wanted, and you'll be a good mother", impregnation could begin! I returned to Jeroen in high spirits.

When we'd 'done it' I stood on my head to allow the sperm to reach my eggs more easily. I got pregnant after 3 months. Briefly it was hard, having had anorexia, and your figure goes crazy! Suddenly you have a belly. I was very pleased with the child in there. I didn't know if it would be a boy or a girl, by then it didn't matter. Every evening for nine months I wrote my unborn baby a letter, about my feelings, longings for the miracle inside me, what I felt when there was contact, movement. I told the baby about myself, who I was as a mother, about Jeroen and us. Before I went to sleep at night I massaged my belly and placed a musical box against it, making contact in that way. The massage was also intended to prevent stretch marks. I wanted to keep my nice smooth belly. I can recommend it!

Being pregnant was both lovely and hard. I was working 40 hours a week, still studying. Also, I experienced the discomforts of pregnancy. When I was heavily pregnant I was given a vibrator for my birthday and a book of sexually-tinted drawings. I refused the presents. Courageous! Jeroen was wonderful during my pregnancy, he never drank alcohol in my presence, was there if I needed him emotionally or physically. He made video films and photos of me in my pregnancy. He was a proud father-to-be. He also accompanied me to antenatal gymnastics classes.

The birth was punishing. They tried to induce it several days in a row, as there was no dilation. By then the baby was three weeks overdue and I'd already been in hospital for a week. On 8 August 1985 a baby girl was born. She immediately recognised the music when I played it to her. I was very happy, over the moon. Sadly, the feeling didn't last long, and I just didn't understand what was going on. Jeroen, with his bar-keeping, arrived home late at night, we were living in a one-room apartment, but that didn't explain why I was so miserable and weepy. It was time, the six weeks were up, I had to return to work and I was paralysed, emotionally. Our daughter went to the crèche for half-day care. I took her and Jeroen collected her. I was on sickness benefit. I hated it, for the second time. Then the company doctor diagnosed a vitamin B deficiency. When that was sorted, I was the happiest of mothers. Right away I switched my family doctor to the company doctor – doctor Felperlaan. From then on, he was my family doctor. I was so grateful to him. Life was no easier. Jeroen worked on Friday evenings and sometimes on Saturdays too. Living as we did in a one-room apartment, it meant I would often be out walking in the park at 7 in the morning, with my daughter in her pram, so we wouldn't disturb Jeroen. I'd been working all week and had to get up early. Not exactly good for my already weary body. In addition, Jeroen had problems accepting his responsibilities and showing initiative.

In the end I had double responsibility, Jeroen continued to enjoy the idle life and was rather lazy – nothing wrong with that as such, but there is if you have a family and a small home. It was a strain on everyone. Yet I did have a good time there, the best in our relationship. I was still unsure of myself sexually, partly because Jeroen didn't know what loving someone meant – love with a capital 'L', making love, sex. We were unable to give each other what we needed. He didn't understand. Jeroen was sex-, not love-orientated. Also, I noticed he was buying condoms and not for me! I was somewhere in Limburg with Jeroen and my mother-in-law and I told her. Her reply: "Never mind" – and that was that.

It wasn't an option to talk 'properly' with Jeroen about it, about the hurt I was feeling. I was worst off, he thought I was inadequate, and that in turn was what I thought of him. I didn't want anyone alongside Jeroen, I wanted him as my partner and the father of my children, and I wanted the same for him.

I was studying hard. I cut back my job from 40 to 32 hours, because it was really hard-going, and I could forgo some hours. Our house, my house, was to be demolished and I wanted to move to a particular neighbourhood where I could buy an old house with a garden, or else rent something there. The housing association came up with two options: rent an old house in one area or new-build in another. We chose the latter. It was what Jeroen wanted and it was close to our work and the crèche … just more practical. Deep down I wasn't impressed, I didn't 'belong' there.

My parents were back together, in fact from the time I got to know Jeroen. They liked him, though they were concerned about the big difference in our backgrounds. I actually considered it to be refreshing. Jeroen's home life was very different: a kind, homespun mother, also avoiding conflict. And a father who, like Jeroen, didn't bear responsibility. Mother worked, father went fishing, played billiards, cycled! Loafing around, he too greatly feared failure, Jeroen had followed suit, but of course it's also in his genes. In that respect, my daughters have my DNA, they've got guts and they pursue success. Jeroen's family didn't really understand my ambition – my ambition as Sylvia. Being a mother was enough, combined with a simple job to earn a bit of money. That caused friction. Then we moved again.

I felt it wasn't an option to have just one child, I wanted an ally for my little girl. A second baby was on its way… again no dilation and so again induced birth. A girl! A happy mother, a happy father, sister, grandpa and grandma. The baby looked like her mum, in terms of behaviour. I saw a small version of Sylvia and knew how to deal with her. There were occasional clashes between Jeroen and the baby. He did his best but was impatient and thought the child was difficult.

Jeroen was increasingly keen to have an 'open' relationship... I started reading books like Wayne W. Dyer's *What Do You Really Want for Your Children,* as well as Louise Hay's *You Can Heal Your Life*. I was very confused. The relationship with Jeroen proved to be a disappointment. I'd thought, always expected that once there was a family he would take more responsibility as a father, and as a partner too. I wanted a career and followed a management course in the evenings. By then I was a qualified orthopedagogue. Again, fulsome praise at my graduation: "an achievement, working, daytime studies and a child!" I felt it wasn't such an achievement. I wasn't pleased! And on graduation day I managed to lose my degree certificate. The cleaner found it in the university loo.

Jeroen wanted an additional relationship, with his ex, and encouraged me to take an additional partner. He never actually did, it was just words. He did stray once or twice but playing around for him was primarily in his imagination – when I was at work or asleep. The tapes awaited him in the broom cupboard.

I wasn't particularly happy with Jeroen as my partner, nor he with me. We couldn't manage to feel the other's pain and help the other to develop. With Jeroen I didn't feel I was the woman I would like to be. And he wasn't the man I wanted beside me. Jeroen was Jeroen, the same one I had fallen for and we were no longer suited. Jeroen: the cheerful, oversexed, irresponsible man as a supportive partner.

I was less and less interested in Jeroen, physically, in the end not in the slightest. We were very open with each other, we had no secrets. Once I went to bed with

Laurence, my married colleague. I was so unsure of myself. With him I felt safe and a woman, and in that way, I confirmed for myself that I was OK. And Laurence was the first man with whom I had an orgasm. When I came home Jeroen asked if I wanted a shower!

I tried to have an affair as well, not to leave Jeroen, but to spice life up a bit. That was my father's advice. He did so want his grandchildren to have parents and not grow up in a broken home. I often thought: if only my parents had parted company I wouldn't have had to go through the misery of their failed marriage.

Deep down I didn't want a 'supplementary' relationship. I wanted to be able to share 'everything' with my partner, with Jeroen, and not get part elsewhere. I badly wanted to give it a chance, so I did my utmost.

I'd reacted to a 'lonely hearts' ad. The wife of the man in question knew about it – at least that's what the ad. said. He turned out to be the psychiatrist of one of my pupils and his wife certainly was not in the know. What an idiot! That was that. I encouraged Jeroen to start studying to become an estate agent. He didn't get much further than a brief case, textbooks and the college fees. He pulled out. We were growing farther and farther apart. My work was tough. I was working in a different department. I was more of a study and psychological mentor of both primary and secondary school children. I was also in charge of intake, I was the Ortho pedagogue. I enjoyed that combination, was good at it and popular. Once during an intake interview, a boy said he only knew my name was Mrs. Duijm. He asked: "Please may I go into Sylvia's group? She's said to be very nice and good at it!" I smiled and told him: "I'm Sylvia". He was extra pleased.

However, I couldn't make a career at the PPIA. I'd once applied for the post of school head and that came to nothing. I understood. I wanted to leave, make a career elsewhere. I applied to the outplacement preparation scheme. With Jeroen as my partner and the little support he gave me I wouldn't cope. I had an offer and if I didn't leave the PPIA, I would have to refund the money. I went to Multi Consult in Haarlem where they advised me I didn't need the scheme – I had guts and talents enough. I was also advised either to leave Jeroen or undergo therapy. I suggested the latter to Jeroen. Initially he didn't feel like it. In the end, we went three times. Then Jeroen said: "Sylvia cramps my style", that was enough for me. He didn't want to make a go of it either. He became a stranger. I worked harder and harder, became skinnier and skinnier, and hyper.

At Multi Consult they had an education expert, Henk. He was also an adherent of Arica, a spiritual group in South America. It turned out that Henk also knew some of Jeroen's friends from Limburg. He was the catalyst that precipitated my final break with Jeroen. He was so different, a good listener, a spiritual man, a good lover and, what I hadn't yet discovered, a very gloomy person and extremely tight-fisted.

I wished it could have been different for my children and myself. Parents who got on well together and radiated that to the children. I tried to imagine how things would be in 5 or 10 years' time. I knew nothing would change. I'd had some good years with Jeroen, confirmed by photographs, yet too little to continue. I didn't want to grow old with him, as my parents had. I wanted Love with a capital letter!

It wasn't easy to find another house. Henk was planning to go to America for a few months and I could live in his flat in Weesp, outside Amsterdam. Jeroen and I were unable to stand sharing a house any longer. He was so cut up, all he wanted was to have me feel unhappy and that doesn't work when you live in the same house. In a shared house you want to see each other being happy. It takes two to tango – I definitely played my part too. We just weren't the perfect match.

I was ill again, had been for the last three months I was with Jeroen, and probably long before that. I thought it was flu, but it didn't pass, and I couldn't afford to be ill. In view of my outplacement, I'd again resigned from one day's work a week, and was still working 24 hours a week at the PPIA. I'd also been taken on as a free-lance communication trainer at the Ministry of Justice for the prison service. Well-paid – 1,000 guilders a day! Contracts signed….

I became even more ill, high fever (40 degrees Celsius, every day, regardless of what I tried), bulging eyes, always hungry, heart pounding, dead tired, looking like a junk, problems sleeping. Great panic attacks, depressed, again wanting to die, again hell. It was agreed with my boss at the PPIA that I should report in sick. I didn't dare to do that for my new freelance job, and he understood. I'd signed contracts and a 'no show' would mean big trouble. I had to pay if I didn't turn up.

Much later, far too late, I was on the verge of a heart attack, I was at hospital having an examination. They wouldn't allow me to leave. I had to stay. I had a severe thyroid complaint and a serious eye infection. I no longer recognised myself, completely lost. You look entirely different when you have an eye infection and your self-esteem is in tatters. Everything I'd built up was shattered. Henk didn't go to America; the trip was off. I stayed in his house, and Jeroen and I shared custody of the children. Henk took good care of me. I fell in love with him, and he took over all my contracts with the prison service, took my children to school in Amsterdam and collected them again. It was not a nice time for my elder girl, a dark chapter in her short life, alongside the divorce. The second child was too young and had a different character. It made less of an impact on her. We stayed in Weesp for nine months. Once I had the right medication, my thyroid gland was working properly again, and my eye disorder was fairly stable, at least for a while. I was back to be the old Sylvia, optimistic, cheerful, feminine and I started to wonder what I was doing in Weesp, in a sixth-floor flat!

I met a conductor, Jacob, a first-class ladies' man with an eye for beauty and quality. We had a short, stormy affair and he spurred me into leaving Weesp and returning to Amsterdam. Agnes, the NXX friend who sometimes used to help me out with marking lessons when I was working in Rotterdam, had bought a house with her partner in Hilversum. Her own home was an apartment in the up-market sector of Amsterdam-South. A splendid, spacious apartment with an attic and a roof terrace – rent 800 guilders (extras excluded). Exactly what I wanted, but actually too much on my salary for 24 hours a week. My father wanted to buy a house for me in The Hague, close to him, but I didn't want to leave Amsterdam. In addition, my parents and sister had discussed my situation behind my back and decided it would be better for my sister and her boyfriend to take care of my children. The children would have family and a 'stabilising factor'! I was furious, and my heart is racing as I write this down. They believed I was unable to take care of myself, let alone my 'girls'.

One day I called on the estate agent who was in charge of the rental of the apartment in Amsterdam. A friend of his was planning to rent it. In the end, thanks to my visits and the fact that his friend considered the apartment too simple, I went to live there. My girls loved the place and its location, 10 minutes by bike to school and a playground in front. I still hadn't fully recovered. Was always weary, my eyes were still bulging and troubling me a lot, I sometimes still had double vision and had to drag myself along. The girls were so sweet to me. One week I would have them for four days, the other for three – the exchange always took place on a Wednesday afternoon. When they had left, I often stood by their beds weeping, the smell of them lingered. They had two sets of everything, so they didn't need to take a case to school. I had a small car and Jeroen could borrow it if he wanted to go somewhere with the girls. When they were with me and the alarm went, my youngest daughter always ran to my small bedroom where I slept in a three-quarter bed. They had the big room, a lovely playroom. She'd dive under my blankets, wanting to re-play 'baby' and her birth. She kept it up for a year, and I did too – she beamed at me when she was being born! She still remembers it. Then, together, the girls made coffee for me, they had to clamber on the counter, and they brought me coffee in bed, always! I took them to school by bike, with the youngest sitting behind me, sometimes by car if cycling was too tiring. I always took the youngest into the classroom, at least until she was in the second form, and gave her a tremendous hug One time I was so ill I had to drop her at the gate. My eldest daughter cycled to school with Bo, a girl from our street. The youngest and I had practised at home – everything she should do and might encounter, as if it were real. By then I had started studying for Practitioner and Master Practitioner NLP (Neuro Linguistic Programming). I helped her to go through everything she should do, in her own mind. In the afternoon I collected her. The teacher called me in and showed me a painting the youngest had made that morning. A self-portrait of a girl with a big smile and a very self-assured look. That painting was an anchor for her, and still is. It hangs in her house.

By then I was receiving disability benefit and considered it awful, beneath my dignity. I definitely could look after myself. I applied for numerous posts. With my appearance – as if I was in a state of constant shock and hyper at the same time – I wasn't of any interest. It was horrible, to be rejected because of the way I looked. I'm crying now, it was such a hard time. Jeroen, the father of my children actually rang me to say the responsibility for them was just too much, and he wanted to end our shared custody. I could have prevented it. Again, life was grim. A woman on her own, and being watched jealously by other women, a possible threat. I had set up my own company, I wanted to get on, and with my NLP training I had something that made me stand out.

No-one really wanted me. I had a few children with learning difficulties whom I helped, a young boy whose father was in prison, a girl who didn't dare to sleep: I understood them and was able to help them. My life was a disaster, financially. Betty needed some domestic help. I went two mornings a week – the place hadn't been properly cleaned for a year. In the afternoons I had acquisitions appointments in Hilton Hotel. Once I had a business dinner with a whole lot of directors. The subject of cleaning ladies cropped up and I described myself, with no-one realising it was about me!

My appearance and double vision were still a drawback. The foremost professor in the Netherlands, possibly in the world, at the Orbita centre of Amsterdam's Academic Medical Centre (AMC) was to operate on me. It entailed decompression surgery: opening up my skull at the hairline to enable the surgeon to reach behind my eye socket. The eyes would be returned to their correct place. An interminable waiting lists. Paula, the assistant, liked me and put me at the top of the list. It was an invasive operation and there was a risk of blindness. When I woke up from the anaesthetic, my father was at my bedside with a spittoon – I puked all over it and lost consciousness again. Lovely, having my father there. I didn't know he would be – the biggest gift he ever gave me: he was there for me! I was longing to see my daughters. My ex complained about the cost of travelling by underground. He was receiving the entire child benefit, but even so. It was hurtful. I promised to pay the fares. My eldest daughter had made a beautiful drawing for me and stuck a 25-cent piece on it. I'd arranged a help group for when I got home again. Carola, Anne and Bert (not Bert from The

Hague) would look after me. They were fellow students from the NLP programme and we got on well together – we used to practise on one another. I couldn't do a thing, and they wouldn't let me. They organised everything for me for a week, ringing when they woke up, shopping, cooking, eating together and cheering me up.

The care they gave me was extraordinary. I soon managed to go to the birthday party for Paula, the professor's assistant. All the doctors who had ever attended to me were there and were amazed that I was walking round, wearing a lovely headscarf (I had no hair on the first 5 centimetres above my hairline). A year later, there was a message from the professor on my answerphone: how was I getting on and if I'd like a date! I never replied. I saw him just once more, for a check-up, and he said: "I rang you. I didn't know if you were having a hard time and wondered if you felt like doing something pleasant". Later I heard he had been having a hard time….

I recovered fairly quickly, the scar was enormous but fortunately my hair covered it a bit. My eyes weren't yet as good as new, still aren't. Another operation on the upper and lower eyelid, the eyes are still different as regards sheathing. Most importantly, I now know and feel that I can once more see my beautiful soul, and the tiny lights. I sometimes forget, and can get myself back on track, telling myself: "Sylvia, I love you", and then I see my soul and the tiny lights, and all is well again.

One day I was in the local Post Office and met my old trainee, Carina, there. She had already been married twice and was heavily pregnant. Like me, she had become a special educator, though not working as such any longer. She was more focused on projects in management and communication, which was gradually becoming my own field. She was working on a project with a partner and they were bogged down. It related to crime prevention in the town Zutphen and was financed by the Ministry of Justice. She brought me on board, and Carina and I were again giving training sessions together, as well as coaching staff from various welfare services involved in the project. My NLP knowledge and experience from the PPIA came in useful. Carina's business partner, a man, had set up a partnership with two others and they called me in, everyone independently. The name of the partnership was Qubus. I had the most diplomas and the smallest network. We were not a unit, one participant dropped out and in the end the partnership died a slow death. I was earning good money and the financial worries were over for a while.

It was a hard time too. When I had to travel to Zutphen, the alarm clock went at 6 a.m., and I took the girls to friends, Anne and Benjamin. Their daughter, Rachel, was in a parallel class to my oldest child. Then on to Zutphen, back home late, pick up the children and take care of them. All too much for someone who was still ill. My thyroid gland started playing up again.

Sometimes I went out. Once with Anne, Rachel's mother. We went to the Molenpad café, but first to the Casino. She wanted to have tried it once. I never went to the Molenpad if I knew Jeroen was working. When Anne and I got there we had fun, a good time. It makes me happy to think back on it. There I met a guy called Kees Jan. He lived on Amsterdam's Prinsengracht. I think we actually danced at the café. We'd arranged for him to pick me up the following Saturday in his Jaguar and go to the beach. It was so enjoyable that I went home with him. The following morning, he had to drive a friend, who was staying with him, to Schiphol airport. The next Saturday was fun too. He'd been married twice, big undertakings, taken a lot of risks as a businessman and was licking his wounds at the time, like me. We didn't become an item, were good friends, and sometimes we did something together with our children. He was nice, had a sense of humour, charming, but not the click you need for a relationship. Jeroen had heard I'd had a good evening out, and he couldn't take it. I was banned from the café. Not allowed in, ever again. Petra, the boss, who was also a friend, dropped me. She didn't make it. She drank and smoked like a chimney. She died of lung cancer. Anne, Rachel's mother, also died of cancer. My youngest daughter told me recently. I was distressed for Benjamin and Rachel, they loved her so much. They were a lovely Jewish family.

I realise that quite a lot of people have gone from my life about whom I haven't written, their destinations unknown. I believe in reincarnation and know I'll meet them again in another life. Sometime.

I had regular assignments. Often teaching in Rotterdam, where I had my school connections. I gave communication training for teachers in the field of team work, ways to improve communication between teachers and students, between teachers and parents, ways to involve parents from ethnic minorities, and so on. I worked with focus and pleasure. Sadly, funds for education were being cut and I was obliged to focus more on profit alongside non-profit. I was asked to arrange a fitting farewell for the Youth Policy Council, which was to be abolished. Together with several other people I organised a series entitled 'education, pleasing or problematic'. I had final responsibility for the content. I had to be in The Hague a lot and come across Tim again (my first boyfriend at secondary school). I'd read in the newspaper that he was the successful director of an international set-up in the art arena, with offices centrally located in The Hague. I rang him, and we agreed to meet for lunch. He kept me waiting for over an hour! It was nice to see him again and he was still as ego-driven as ever. I couldn't get a word in edgeways! We arranged to meet again in Amsterdam and he invited me to celebrate New Year's Eve at his brother Roel's place: the two of them would be organising a party.

By then I had got my Master Practitioner NLP degree. It turned out I was also good at bringing in students for the various programmes, as well as teaching. I discussed it with my trainer Eric and decided to do the course for international trainer NLP and become his assistant. I was already giving introduction training. The first was to be in New York. I decided right away, bought my ticket, ran up a few debts. It was investment in my future. I had got to know Francine at the NLP course and she is now one of my best friends. She wanted to join the study group, which had cared for me so well after my operation. Something went wrong: we should have met at my place, but I had to cancel because of a migraine, and I'd completely forgotten about Francine. She rang the front door bell, she came upstairs and introduced me to Reiki. It is a form of hands-on healing transferring energy from practitioner to patient. She felt the tension in my head. I told her: "I feel so alone, so lonely." She claims I also said I really wanted a partner – I'd been on my own for two years. I've forgotten but do believe her. The migraine faded. Francine continued to give me Reiki now and then and I was her first paying customer. We were both very pleased about it. Since then I have got my I and II level certificates under her sister Glenny.

New Year's Eve of 1995 was imminent. Jeroen had taken the two girls in my car to Petra, owner of the Molenpad, to her home in Broek in Waterland. I'd decided to stay home, nice and quietly on my own. I'd celebrate the arrival of the New Year in the bath with champagne and salmon, and a syllabus of assignments for the course in New York to which I was going the next week. Things turned out differently. At about 9 p.m. the phone rang: it was Tim. Did I want to go to a party he and his brother Roel were organising? Well, if he rang specially I must be very welcome! There was a green dress I'd had someone make for me. I put it on, with gorgeous, green high heels and my hold-up stockings. Ready to party! Accompanied by a bottle of champagne and some nuts, on my bike to the party.

It was a huge building. It looked imposing on the outside and like a squat inside. At least, that was my first thought. Big rooms, high ceilings, lots of rooms. Indeed, too large to be really perfect. A 300 square-metre house in Amsterdam's inner city. Other than Tim and Roel, I knew no-one at the party. I make contacts easily and I soon noticed Tim couldn't give me much attention. His Spanish girlfriend kept a close watch on him, he was allowed to be there for her and her alone. It was very strange – the host not being permitted to have anything to do with you. Roel proved to be a different kind of host: he showed me round the house and in the attic of the back part of the house we must have sat talking for an hour about boarding school – he'd spent four years in one and also had also done middle school 'MULO', having dropped out of grammar school. We spoke about our parents: I knew his from the past, about the St. Jan's college, which we'd both attended. We talked and talked. The other guests (so I heard later) thought we'd been screwing in the attic! We hadn't touched each other, we were so deep in conversation.Back at the party, Roel told me that Tim had come to live there too. I remarked: "Gosh, imagine you get a girlfriend, I don't think that would work". I didn't know Roel actually had a girlfriend – it wasn't apparent that evening.Later I discovered she had been at the party too. At about midnight we went up to the top of the front part of the house where the refurbishment for Tim was in full swing. Roel grabbed his jacket from the hook and wrapped it round me against the cold. Wow, what a gentleman! He knew which was my bottle of champagne and he was the first person with whom I toasted the New Year at midnight. Stayed until 7 in the morning and then cycled back home. I had a feeling I was home – at home with Roel! That morning I was sitting like a deflated balloon when Jeroen brought the children. He saw something had happened to me and I told him I'd got home at 7 a.m. That wasn't like me and Jeroen realised he'd lost me for good. He'd been secretly hoping I'd go back to him. His anger and distress returned.

That Monday evening, I rang Roel and got the answering machine. I left a message: "Was it real or was it a dream on New Year's Eve?" That evening he returned my call. He'd wanted to ring me first, but he'd stayed on in the pub – that much was evident!

We arranged to meet that Friday. It was snowing, a romantic day. I was happy and Roel told me later that he'd walked to work that morning, dancing through the snow – so happy, he felt like a dancing snowflake. We arranged to meet in the same pub where I'd had my first drink with Jeroen. I had two Camparis with ice and a slice of orange, and Roel had a couple of beers. He proved overly fond of his beer. We went on for a meal at a Nepalese restaurant, and then to Roel's favourite bar. I've never been a pub-crawler and it was all a bit much. I stuck to water, I couldn't face more alcohol.

Roel was still half in a relationship, it had been on the line for six months. The following day they broke up permanently as a couple but were still friends. Then, at about 2 a.m. Roel came around. I was asleep. I picked my girls up the next day and Roel and I took them sledging, I had two sledges. I took the oldest and Roel the youngest. Then we had pancakes at the Amsterdamse Bos park. That day was pronounced one to be repeated every year! Roel and I got together. My youngest daughter of 6 was very fond of him, my oldest – 9 years old by then – did not get on well with Roel. She didn't want another man for her mother, she wanted Papa and Mama.

I went to New York and had a wonderful week there. I made the acquaintance of the late President Roosevelt 's granddaughter who was also following the programme for international trainer. I spent a night on her couch. We'd both had quite a bit to drink! The next morning, I took a taxi to the exam, she pulled out. With my stomach in my head and my head in my stomach I gave a speech in English. No-one caught on. Clearly, I'm pretty good at functioning when I have to – regardless!

Roel was supposed to pick me up at Schiphol airport. He'd rung me every evening in my hotel room in New York. I was proud, someone was collecting me, and I envisaged Roel standing there with flowers, so happy to take me in his arms. But… no Roel! He was over an hour late. My fellow passengers, whom I had already prepared to witness my romantic encounter, had all left. Roel had forgotten where he'd left his car. He'd been out on the tiles the night before and had gone to bed far too late. Ouch! I didn't understand. If I were to arrange to pick my beloved up, I would have gone through it ten times in my mind beforehand. Like making my own film. Alcohol continued to be an issue, it shifts your boundaries. Roel often cancelled appointments – staying too long at work, hanging round in the pub. It was hard to cope with, that 'interference', those undercurrents. By then I was wise to it! I stopped my international trainer-ship. My relationship with Roel was mainly one for the weekends, the children were often around on Sundays too. I was still not completely on track, time and again my thyroid gland started playing up. I didn't want to be a trainer. It often meant working at weekends. I wanted to do more therapeutic work, really getting down to the root of things with clients – which you do with coaching. Occasionally I doubted my abilities as a trainer. Was I good enough? There were so many people better at it!

Now I'm better at assessing myself. Sure, there will be people with better training skills. I know better than anyone that my forte is my ability to kindle enthusiasm, to motive people to go all out for something. Once I had to teach a class a song as part of the exam for the NXX course. I didn't have a clue. Beating time and sticking to the rhythm – it was a big mess. However, the examiners (there were three) told me: "You've passed with flying colours. They haven't learnt the song, but the most important thing is that that you made them enthusiastic for singing. There's no better experience!" I recall that when I doubt my abilities.

Roel had a large house and mine was small in comparison. He lived practically round the corner from his work opposite 'his' bar. I hoped that if we did decide to live together, he wouldn't be so keen to pass though the pub on the way home. I wanted to share a house with him. It was somewhat less important for Roel, though he had meanwhile had the house remodelled so there were two children's rooms. The children were allowed to have their say, as long as it was structurally feasible. The 'squatter' section was also improved. I had a lot of influence in the revamp. Tim had moved in as well, he had his own loft space. He'd created a splendid apartment, a huge, luxury make-over. The best 100-square metre space in the whole house! Tim often did things without prior consultation and acted as if everything belonged to him, taking what he needed or thought he did, took no-one into consideration and was expert at disturbing Roel's and my privacy. Roel gave him more than enough scope for that. He'd just break off a conversation between the two of us about unpleasant things that needed our attention – it was all about Tim, his fortunes. Roel felt responsible for his younger brother and also for his two exes, who came to parties, one of whom often misbehaved. She clung to Roel, demanded his complete attention, sat on top of him as if he were her partner. She managed to come between us and Roel allowed it to happen. His argument was that I was moaning, I was strong enough, the others were vulnerable. I didn't succeed in showing and explaining to him that I was indeed strong, but it was hurtful and not normal. Apparently, I was never satisfied and always had to criticise or get attention. True, particularly the latter. I did – still do – give the other party leeway. Sometimes it's necessary, if I'm wrapped up in something. OK, but don't bash someone emotionally!

Roel and I moved in together. I cancelled my tenancy and made sure a mother who wanted to leave her husband could live in my house with her daughter, a small girl in my daughter's class. I'm not someone who wants to give something a trial run – it's all or nothing! After a week, my daughter said: "Mum, why did we come to live here, Roel's never home." I gulped. She was right. Nothing had changed. The pub was more important than home. And my thyroid was playing up again. The plan was to treat it with radioactive iodine, the doctors wanted my thyroid gland to shrink and not work so hard. The risk being that if you swallow too much it can have the opposite effect: you become lethargic, fatter and confused. Roel took me to the nuclear radiation department of Amsterdam Academic Hospital (AMC) hospital. I wore clothes that could be thrown away afterwards.

I had a room with a phone and television. I had to lie in bed. A man wearing a protective white 'lunar' suit and a mask entered my room with a huge machine containing a small box, with another small box inside, with a stick fitted with a hand that gave me a pill – I had to swallow it with a glass of water. I wasn't scared. Every couple of hours the man in the protective suit returned with a Geiger counter to measure radioactivity. The following day, towards evening, I was allowed to go home. Roel collected me. We were happy to see each other. We'd spoken a lot on the phone. The clothes were incinerated, and I wasn't allowed to go near babies for an entire month. Roel and I had a jolly time together. The other side of the coin. According to my younger daughter we sometimes behaved like two big kids larking around. We could really enjoy ourselves and laughed a lot when we did things together. We travelled a lot, mainly eastwards, Roel didn't like to go in the direction of America. Once we stayed in a three-star hotel, two-stars would have even been too much. In the middle of the night I climbed up a wall via Roel's shoulders and removed one star. What a lark! Another time, in Egypt at the Red Sea – I was in a crazy mood, took off my dress and threw it in the air. I didn't catch it and it landed at the bottom of the sea. Roel in pursuit. And another time I crossed the Nile as a stowaway in a boat full of tourists – there was no other boat available at the time. Discovered and thrown off! I could write a book about our adventures. Unfortunately, there was often 'interference', Roel's irritation, aggravated by alcohol. Even on the first evening of our honeymoon. We got married on his 50th birthday, I was his present, after 5 years together. Roel had proposed on New Year's Eve 2000 – five years after we'd met. We had a Royal Wedding. I'd organised everything, from the wedding venue in the Tropenmuseum [Tropical Institute] to the party in the Hortus Botanicus [botanical garden]. I'd commissioned a gorgeous outfit with matching hat, the girls were also dressed in bespoke clothing – they were allowed to choose the design and material themselves, though both had to wear the same fabric – which required some teamwork! It was an incredible wedding. First married to Jeroen for free on a Monday morning at 9 a.m., more of a formality because we wanted children. The day after the Royal Wedding we went to Limburg, where we stayed in a small castle (which I'd also arranged). Roel was busy with work and thought the way I'd gone about it was fine. His father died six weeks before the wedding. Sadly. He had liked me! He often said something like "You graduated in love". I cut his hair and was always solicitous for Roel's father and mother. The room in the castle was a disappointment, not as romantic as in the photo – and I said so. At such times Roel felt I was dissatisfied. But all I wanted was to mention it and that was that. But that's not the way it worked. A room, romantic surroundings, it was so important. For Roel what mattered was beer or the like. He felt and actually said that I, Sylvia, was never satisfied. Out for dinner in Maastricht, dreadful weather! I really don't like driving at night, I can't see too well, so Roel was to drive. A few glasses of beer and wine, and Roel wanted a brandy. I suggested waiting with the brandy until we were back in the hotel, since we had to drive in bad weather – not even saying the amount he'd had to drink was too much for someone driving in such conditions. It ended in a terrific row. Those undercurrents ran through our relationship. I became uncertain – what could I say, or not? Roel also often came home late from the pub – he forgot the time when he was there. It was hard to discuss my feelings, my fears, our undercurrents, his behaviour. He thought I should stop feeling insecure. He'd dealt with everything. I was stuck in old traumas…

If Roel didn't have a meeting or was at the pub, he often had to work late. One time I hid his briefcase, I wanted some attention for once. I also used my infamous 'light therapy' on occasions. If Roel wanted to sleep I switched the light on again, I wanted to talk. He switched the light off, I switched it on again. It didn't improve the situation. I could be really nasty.

Roel worked for a time in Wageningen in the central Netherlands. He always had financial jobs, as the financial boss. As he says: "always at the top of my career!" I often collected him from the station when the children were with their father. I enjoyed seeing how he walked through the crowds with their bags and their concerns, and when he saw me he'd come towards me, beaming. We often went for a drink or bite in the centre of Amsterdam. Happy memories!

Work in Wageningen wasn't easy, Roel worked long hours. Up early. I was always up first, very conventional, making coffee and preparing breakfast. Always, for my two girls too. They often took the tram to school, I took them to the tram stop outside the Bijenkorf department store and was waiting for them there after school. When they were a bit older, they went by bike. I had work in Amsterdam again. Roel would often take our youngest to school, cycling together. Roel was extremely fond of her before she was an adolescent.

At some stage I joined the Women's Network of Amsterdam – a network of highly-qualified professional women, with top jobs or their own companies. I had set up Duijm Consultants, a company addressing educational and change processes. I don't know how I got in. I had to give a talk and based on that and several other criteria would be invited to join. I got in! I did quite a lot for the network, giving talks, and networking worked in my favour for assignments. Now, 20 years later, I'm still a member, and have held all kinds of positions, from leader to member of a group to hold the organisation together, to chair of the whole club. Each year I plan to resign and then I allow myself to be persuaded to stay on. No persuasion this year – other priorities! When there was a network meeting Roel was supposed to return early to cook for the children, read them a story and put them to bed. It often didn't turn out that way and, in the end, I only went to meetings when they were at their father's. My life had shrunk, and I really wasn't really happy. Expectations had flown. Again, I felt insecure, no longer liked myself and so felt less attractive. Work was tough going as well, I had my hands full coping with the relationship between Roel and the girls. Particularly the older daughter, who had never chosen to live with him. I felt I was in the middle of a sandwich. She started to spend more time at her father's. Tim's presence made matters no easier. We lived in the same house for almost 8 years and he never actually knew the children's names. I regularly talked to my mother about my relationship and my unhappiness. She had the standard reaction: "We all have our cross to bear and Roel means well". Result: I continued to try to please.

For her entire life my mother had defended her relationship with my father and I couldn't blame her. I just hoped if I got away from the house, away from Tim (who would also have to leave if the place was sold), life would become more enjoyable, more open and friendly. That I would also have a new house where everything worked. Roel always wanted to mend everything himself, though he wasn't all that good at it. For six months we had a bath in the corridor! There was often something wrong. I kept on hoping, making an effort, proving willing, perhaps against my better judgement, yet that was how I was. Roel did his best too. As he put it: he adored me. He'd never wanted children, but he would have liked one with me. Financially Roel ensured we lacked for nothing. I wanted a country cottage for the family and we had one built in the Czech Republic. Early on, my youngest daughter would go with us, with some of her friends. She was also troubled by Roel's 'interference' and unpredictability. It made it all so much more awkward. We weren't on the same page as regards sharing our emotions and ideas. Roel and I both ended up single and the family home didn't become a home for the family. Today it's up for sale!

Neither Roel nor I had been brought up to share our feelings and what was taking place deep within us. Nor had our parents learned how to, and so they were unable to pass it on. Yet I have succeeded in developing it, by looking around myself and also thanks to my therapies and studies. Sadly, not together with him! I grew apart from Roel. By then we had moved from the city centre to the neighbourhood of Zeeburg. I wanted to get away – away from people urinating in public, the trafficking in women, tipsy Brits and – in particular – my brother-in-law Tim. Tim could go on living in Roel's house until his death, even if Roel were to die first. My youngest daughter also wanted to move from the house where there always some 'issue', materially or emotionally. Roel bought a lovely place along the Amsterdam-Rhine canal. I knew it was in fact just for me and for her. He didn't feel the need to move.

The modern house had two living sections, front and back, a carport and a terrace. My house at Oudezijds was hard to sell, it took three years. It was 300 square metres, in a less salubrious part of the city, and had to make good money. It was a huge expense. I kept part of the house as an office where I could give courses. I wanted to let part as a Bed & Breakfast, and part to other freelancers. In the end I managed to let it on a temporary basis, to foreign lecturers, via the Rijksacademie. Some special encounters resulted. It was a good thing there was more income, as Roel had triple expenses. Those worries were not exactly conducive to a pleasant life together. Roel didn't want to split the expenses either, nor see if I could help out financially. We were not a team. I was proud that I had finally succeeded in letting the house. If I did manage to let the house, I'd have a weekend in Istanbul, because on a previous visit we'd done nothing but take taxis and get wet feet – four days of non-stop downpours! The weekend never materialised. Roel thought my letting the house had been a piece of cake.

His father's death also had repercussions for our relationship. There was quite a bit of money. Moreover, Roel was made redundant on account of a reshuffle at work, with a different kind of management. He was at the peak of his career. There was no chance of something very different, just a similar post in a different municipal service. Roel planned to invest his capital well and focus on asset management as a job. I encouraged him, hoping we would have more time for each other, go to the Czech Republic more often, have more fun. I also hoped that in time we could set up some joint projects, like an orphanage in Nepal or India. So Roel would deploy his financial know-how and I would focus on special education. It was all fine with me as long as we were creating something wholeheartedly and of course with the necessary expertise. The very opposite occurred. We often sat in separate rooms. I had meanwhile done a postgraduate course for ZKM (self-confrontation method) coach and was fully absorbed in it. It proved to be 'the way' to bring to the surface underlying convictions as to why people do something, or not, what stimulates them and what holds them back. You discover the emotional pattern beneath the life pattern. I learnt a lot about myself as a result and managed to open up for myself the road to love.

That method got me quite a few assignments, also through my women's network. The original idea was to focus initially on ex-pats, both those coming to the Netherlands and those (Dutch) posted abroad. It was interesting for me too, as the daughter of an ex-pat! Often when you work in and with a different culture, you settle back into your own weaknesses and pitfalls. Unfortunately, the companies that were supposed to set up this joint project did not succeed in getting off the ground due to a lack of cooperation. I did get a very good friend, Riky, out of it, and her husband, who belonged to one of the organisations in question; he became a good friend too. Not that he was involved in setting up the project, he was more geared to intercultural management.

Roel and I were never able to build a bridge between our worlds. Our friends and families were separate too. As soon as we moved in together, I invited the whole crowd for my birthday – Roel's friends and relations. I wanted a big 'do', inside and out. There was no spin-off. The worlds stayed apart. Every attempt to have a convivial dinner ended in me commanding all the attention. There was no room for anyone else.

My youngest daughter went to live with her father early on. She and Roel clashed tremendously: she is behaving like an adolescent and he counter-reacting. All very painful and at the time I just couldn't manage to take a strong stance. I was scared and tried to pacify them, as my mother once did. Horrible, in situations like that you must react with your heart, stand up for what you truly believe – and say so. I'd start that way…and then got lost. I was no match for Roel's anger and aggression and nor was my youngest daughter. It still makes me weep. My greatest wish was to give my children the love and support I had lacked so much, and I failed as a mother in that respect. Dismally. My daughter's departure damaged the relationship between Roel and myself severely. I wanted to go with him in therapy. Learn to work together, learn to communicate with each other. Roel didn't want to. I went to therapy again myself, hoping that if I changed, if I were stronger, things would be different, we'd get closer to each other again and perhaps have my daughters back with us. It didn't work out.

I became progressively happy about myself, started meditating, …reacting more and living from the heart.

Roel would sometimes react very sarcastically: "Did you learn that nonsense in a course?" When I went to yoga, he remarked: "I'd rather you had cookery lessons!" I think the moment my youngest daughter left was the point of no return.

By then my mother was old and sick, she had Parkinson's disease. I often took care of her, went for walks with her, spoilt her. She really looked forward to my visits, phone calls and letters. Roel was very fond of my mother and often went with me. We also sometimes looked after her for a weekend to give my father some space. In the end, my mother died in my arms. There were two things I said to her as she was drawing her final breaths:

"Mum, you were a good mother, and I'm going to stop pleasing – I'm giving it back to you." When I was clearing out her handbag, I found in it a letter I'd written – that was all. A letter containing wise advice, encouraging, explaining how she could make the best of her illness, her fears and my not very empathetic father.

At last we had found each other. Her death was a step towards my liberation.

My mother's passing led to some big changes. I inherited statutory portion, and all of a sudden, I had € 80,000 in my bank account.Passed some on to my daughters to fulfil financial desires that normally were beyond them. Went to Africa with Roel. I wanted to put the money to good use and not let it fester in the bank. We needed a new car; the house needed a revamp. Roel didn't want any money from me for anything whatsoever.

I had met a couturier, I modelled in a fashion show for him and actually wanted to fulfil a burning desire. It may sound arrogant, but I was often the best dressed woman at my work in Rotterdam, later at the PPIA. The women in my network always asked where I got my clothes. I thought a lot of it up myself, buying the material and having it made up. What could be better than working with a couturier and, as a networker, marketing it myself, being able to influence the designs. I can sew a bit, learned it from Babs my neighbour when I was a child, later I had sewing lessons at the school of fashion. I knew nothing about making patterns. This could be an excellent joint venture…

I had money. However, the plan to join forces with the couturier was a disaster. He didn't stick to any of our agreements. He failed to turn up at one big event where we were meant to be promoting ourselves. Fortunately, I'm quite good at improvising. It turned out that he was very insecure and that resulted in a 'no show'!

By then my American girl friend had arrived in Holland for a reunion of our primary school (filmed for the TV programme 'Hello Goodbye'). She met my daughters and they got on well. The youngest had started her History studies. I, and everyone else envisaged problems before she'd even started, but she particularly wanted to study that subject. My motto is, you have to have the experience yourself and sometimes you have to pay dearly. Yet, when you bring up children, you must know how far to go, and sometimes decide that the solution is to let go. With safety as the foremost criterion. She stuck to her studies for two months. Yoze invited her to California as an au pair. She would arrange a family. No sooner said than done. My youngest went to America. I visited her there, paid for it myself, and we went on a wonderful trip with Yoze, her sister, my daughter and me. Yoze likes luxury, so every indulgence. I could afford it. Great! We laughed so much, had so much fun, no 'interference'. I missed Roel, yet I didn't. No comment!

Back in the Netherlands I broke off for good with the couturier and continued on my own. I found a sewing atelier, a pattern maker, a template maker for printing patterns on cardboard – really old-fashioned, reliable patterns, a website designer, the right fabric supplier, a photographer, models, a label company, lids for boxes, labels, zips and everything you need to put together two-piece suits – and that's a lot! As a layperson, you don't realise. In other words, an entire company, into which all my money vanished. And I almost drowned. I'd bought an Alpha Spider V6 to transport all the necessities. Unfortunately, not everything went in, and the car was expensive to run. Yet I loved my car.

I had too much and too little know-how, everyone was earning a lot off me, and I was earning nothing. Resources exhausted. Roel just looked on. According to him, I wasn't badly off, but the people I wanted to break with were, for instance the sewing atelier because production was below the mark. I felt awful, so many nice people worked there, but my critical eyes noticed the flaws. They couldn't meet my standards and I had too little expertise to do it for them. We couldn't tango together! Roel was no comfort, he sided with the atelier, they were losing a client.

Francine, my Reiki friend, had a friend who was a seamstress. She saved me from downfall. She discovered that the bust darts on the patterns were wrong. I could see something wasn't right, but not exactly why. All the patterns had to be changed, the entire collection was substandard. The photo shoots had to be repeated. Riky from the ZKM course was delighted to help out. Together we made the first professional look-book of all the photos with descriptions. The flaws were also visible in the photos. New patterns, new models, a new book and a new name 'Deux Pièces by Sylvie D.

My big dream was to have my two businesses cross-pollinate. LLC, life career coaching, formerly Duijm consultants, and Deux Pièces. Two sides of the same coin. LLC would ensure a powerful 'inside' and Deux Pièces the outside. However, clients opt for one angle. A workshop, yes, but not the clothing, and vice versa. OK. The companies are still there, happily side by side!

I wanted too much. I was working day and night. I loved it, but Roel felt let down. I know if all had been well between us I would never have taken that step. A step causing estrangement rather than rapprochement. For me 'a loving relationship' is my first priority. I truly wish for that with Erik, Erik the love of my life, to whom I have dedicated this book, alongside my daughters.

Increasingly Roel had to travel alone to the Czech Republic, or elsewhere. I had no time. I could manage one or two weeks, but Roel wanted to go for longer.

My fabric supplier proved to be a special person, very spiritual, a university education, well-read and splendid charisma. I had to buy a lot of fabrics, I was told it was important to have a large stock (as some might be sold out later) for my production, and at the right price. I visited my fabric supplier every week and once I'd acquired all I needed, I was sad not to see him anymore. As I drove away I realised how much I would miss him. Purchases over, we always drank coffee together and had lovely, profound conversations.He also cheered me up, and I him. When I was with Roel I'd never allowed another man to get close, didn't want to. Roel was my husband and I was faithful, and vice versa. When I got home I sent the 'fabric man' a card, saying: "Instead of taking leave in a cool and rather clumsy way, I would prefer to call round for a coffee now and then, without having to buy anything!" But a couple of weeks later, I'd run out of something and had to return to my fabric supplier. He took me into darker and darker places in the building and suddenly he grabbed hold of me and kissed me, like in the film *Gone with the Wind*. I thought I'd faint, the fire, the passion, overwhelming, and my complete surrender. We were one!

Yet another catalyst. I had felt something I'd always wanted to feel and would never feel with Roel. With him I always felt something keeping me back, as was the case with Jeroen. Now, for the first time uninhibited…

I was feeling more and more feminine with Roel and noticed it when I looked at myself: on the outside, I looked more feminine and acted accordingly. On the inside it was more about wanting to feel feminine, a lack of 'having got there'. It was also evident in my sexual behaviour with Roel. I made love more with my will than my emotions. For instance, I'd hear a little voice saying: "It's time to make love" or "Making love brings you closer together". And then I'd add deeds to words. But if the electricity is lacking, you have sex not true love. I had talked to Roel about it, that an emotional bond is a precondition for a loving relationship. His criticism of me and the concomitant rejection made it impossible for me to bond emotionally with him (any longer). At some stage Roel said: "I think the magic between us has vanished". He was right. I can't remember exactly when it happened. I do know that my encounter with the 'fabric man' was responsible – the final straw that broke the camel's back. Also, that man's energy and encouraging attitude. He was married and was not my husband. But I'd tasted and felt what it did to me. A lot!

I found an advertisement for workspace in an old school, combined with a pied-à-terre. I phoned. The woman on the phone asked why I wanted to rent the space. I answered briefly: "I want to leave my husband". My reaction was so spontaneous, I'd never said it before. Frequently felt it. I often thought if only I were living in a little attic – nice and alone and safe. Safe, loving towards myself without repeated comments about all the things that were wrong with me. I had talked about it with my girlfriends. My daughters also saw how unhappy I was, and everyone thought: "She'll never go, she'll never leave her comfort zone. She's too well off, materially".

Roel was in Romania with a friend when I answered the advertisement. Riky helped me take out the modular ceiling in the work space to create a high room, and I could build a mezzanine floor where I could sleep. I'd made a drawing of how I wanted it. We hadn't laughed so much in years. It was like a James Bond film. We were disguised with masks and caps, and the ceiling was a risk too. It would have cost 1000 euros to have someone do it for me. Once the ceiling was out, I said: "I don't want to go on. It doesn't feel right. The time isn't ripe yet!" Riky understood and thanked me for the adventure and the fun we'd had. The lady who was renting the space understood too. Happy the ceiling had gone. Also, I'd run out of money, my inheritance had been spent on my company, the rent was stiff, and it didn't feel right! That's what it's all about – feelings. I wasn't ready for it.

A year later I awoke feeling an angel had touched me, saying: "Sylvia, now's the time to go!" I started to cry and told Roel I was leaving. It had been mentioned before and Roel thought, she'll never do it. I told him: "I'll put it on the back burner and see what happens". I was wretched, I loved Roel but wasn't happy, and knew I'd never find peace, happiness and passion with that man. We went to the beach together, and it seemed like the early days. But of course, it wasn't. I still went to Thailand with him. He went two weeks ahead of me. He collected me from the airport. I couldn't see him and the old feeling I'd had when I returned from NY surfaced (when he wasn't there, and I had waited for him expectantly). Roel texted me, he couldn't get any closer. I saw him and looked in his eyes, and knew this isn't my husband, with that look. The trip was a big disappointment, particularly for Roel. Very awkward.I drew men's attention right away, there was no perceptible bond between Roel and me – in fact, there hadn't been for a long time.

Back in Holland I was certain. I had to leave him. We had to get a divorce. Each of us build up a life of our own. We were still young. My 'beloved' car, my Alfa Spider with its V6 engine, had to go. I would have to live in a so-called 'anti-squat'. That was all I could afford. Roel and I had a prenuptial agreement, with exclusion of all community of property. I went to my Alfa dealer and good friend Pascal, telling him: "My car has to be sold.

I'm going to live in an anti-squat. I'm leaving Roel". He asked if I'd already found somewhere to live. I told him I hadn't, but I was bound to succeed. He took the phone and rang someone. When he put the phone down he said: "I've found somewhere for you through a friend. On the Keizersgracht canal. You can go and look at it now. They're expecting you".

Around six o'clock on Good Friday 2011 I left on my bike, with my bag. My friend Francine (Reiki) was standing on the corner and took me to my new quarters. I was shattered. Wretched, but also very proud and cautiously pleased that I'd take that step and hadn't acted as everyone expected – she won't do it, give up her comfort! My heart had become my guide, and still is. Free for love!

Free to love

Free to love A few days ago it was my birthday and it's already three years since I left Roel. There was a birthday card from him in my letter box. He wished me a nice day and a year filled with happiness and contentment, ending with 'yours for ever'.

Distressing, painful, sad. Roel is still in the drama triangle, he's not happy…

I feel free to love and Roel is captive in his love for me! He's profoundly miserable, he's lost the woman with whom he wanted to grow old and whom he truly loved. Those thoughts have a fierce grip on him. The woman he loved has changed. She changed from a dependent woman, depending on someone's love, into a woman who loves herself dearly and also knows what true love is – and that is not what Roel gave her. A woman who also has plenty of room love for and from the other person. But there is one difference. Love starts with loving myself. I now know what love with a capital letter means. Unconditional love. Unconditional based on yourself and based on the other. With space and freedom. Free to grow over time and the space you need.

I do not want any other kind of love, it's not possible for me! Not that it's easy. I grew up expecting to please, practically buying love, and adjusting and hoping things would change, full of expectations, often against my better judgement. I'm not only skilled in special education but am a 'hands-on' expert too! Our ego, our personality often gets in the way.

Back to the time of the 'anti-squat'. I went there with no expectations. I just wanted things to 'happen', not a tsunami, but like a wave that you touch and anticipate. I'm done with expectations. Expectations lead to disappointments – over and done with! It's about trust. Deep down I had trust and it's only increased. Trust that the universe takes good care of me. That I get what is best for me at that particular moment.

Oddly enough – or perhaps not – I had almost the same feeling as when I started boarding school, my new kind of living. The feeling of being let down. A very similar sense of being abandoned. The first evening my friend Francine left me, lovingly, with my small bag, at a special place near the '9 little streets' at Keizersgracht canal. Actually, a place where you start out as a student – and that was long behind me.

True, I'd let Roel down, but I felt he had done the same with me: "You, Roel, let me down by not wanting to develop with me!" I thought, sometimes angrily, sometimes weeping. When my ego got the upper hand... Someone once said: "Syl, Roel doesn't know what it means to love someone, Roel knows what it is to have."

The first week I was really shattered. I cried myself to sleep, as I had at boarding school. Sleeping on an Ikea bed settee in a dusty room where windows didn't open, alone in bed. I'd shared a bed for sixteen years: it was a liberating but lonely feeling.

My friends Francine and Riky helped me really well and lovingly through those early days. Riky primarily in a practical way, Francine primarily emotionally. Francine would ring in the morning to invite me for breakfast somewhere. We did that for almost half the first week. I often ate at Riky's place, to start with lunch on Easter Sunday. Riky is a great help with painting, packing and moving to a new house!

The place where I was living was a completely different world, entirely different surroundings and entirely different people from those I was accustomed to being with. There were also rules I hadn't thought about to start with, and inevitably, almost a week later I was thrown out. My room was a wooden 'space' measuring 70 square metres, on the ground floor with large windows overlooking the canal. There was a wooden closet in a corridor, with a curtain: it was the toilet, and beside it there was a shower.Adjoining it, an open space (open to the toilet via the ceiling) with a kitchen unit, then my own electric cooking ring on a table, and a washing machine which I was allowed to use – that was the kitchen. The walls were made of crumbling bricks, not insulated, and you could see all the floors above (and there were a lot!) through a hole. Everything was basic, so basic, yet I didn't experience it as such – I'm now thinking from the present, looking back. I was profoundly happy with my safe place. A place without criticism, without passive and active aggression. Although…

It was the Queen's Birthday, a public holiday when people can sell pretty well anything in the street. I'd just moved in. Awesome, living in the city centre. I invited my sister and some friends. Put tables and chairs on the street, making an entire shop with clothes and shoes I didn't wear any more. Indoors people could try things on in front of a mirror. Being a kind person, I allowed them to go to the loo on the first floor – for free, of course. At the end of the day we planned to eat and drink outdoors, But then!

Then the caretaker arrived and asked if I was out of my mind, if I knew what my duties were. To ensure no strangers went indoors. Anti-squat. Oops, I'd completely forgotten. Furious – I could move out next day. My sister put in a good word for me, and I did too, and in the end we 'made up'. It was a lovely, loving feeling, my sister sticking up for me and explaining what I was like: enthusiastic and forgetting what it was all about. I lived there for 18 months. All the occupants had their own story, a life story filled with pain, disappointment, struggling back: a temporary refuge towards happiness or further down the slippery slope. For me it was the refuge towards happiness.

A baby was even born in the anti-squat house. Wonderful. I was allowed to cuddle the little one now and then, even babysat occasionally. She lay in my bed and I lay beside her, gently stroking her, with music by Mozart in the background. That is when you know and feel what love is – so tiny, so innocent, in a bare, cold building. It calms you and lets you 'flow'.

You needed that feeling in the winter. I experienced one there, almost unbearable. Everything froze in the kitchen, going to the loo was a disaster, your pee steamed, and taking a shower was Spartan! Also, my room was impossible to heat.

Then you realise how spoiled we are and what a hard life some people have when doomed to live that way. It was a temporary measure for me, as well as an adventure.

An adventure, a quest to rediscover the self-love I was convinced I'd once had. I started by putting on my desk a photo of myself as a three-year old. That girl was so radiant, so loving, so open, so playful: she looked trustingly out into the world – 'the fool child'! I made contact with that girl each day. I wanted to be her again, on the inside, with my adult self on the outside.

I'd done sports all my life, important for my figure and even more important for my strong spirit and splendid energy. I'd already been going to Charles where he worked at Krasnapolsky Hotel, and prior to that when he was at Barbizon Hotel. I often went with my father when he was alive (by then 86 years old and living in Baarn). It was nice and lavishly appointed, and I could afford it. And thanks to the low anti-squat rent of 150 euros, I could continue to afford it. Unlimited keep-fit with Charles cost the same as my rent. Sometimes my father paid for me. His feelings were dualistic. He was both worried, but proud, that, at her age, his youngest daughter was living in an anti-squat place, proud because I'm stubborn and took full responsibility for leaving Roel. My daughters liked to join me in my new home, though the eldest had some problems with my nomadic existence. My sister loved staying in the centre of the city. We celebrated St. Nicolas evening there – my father and his lady friend Truus, my sister, my daughters and their father Jeroen. When I first lived there I went for my workout with Charles almost every morning. My body was broken by emotion and I slept badly. The yoga exercises I learned from Charles got the flow back in my body, and so helped with healing. The sadness and tension could drain away. I gradually began to feel stronger physically and emotionally. Movement is my cure for regaining strength – it generates flow. Body and soul as one. The relaxation in my body brought about the flow and my spirit became calmer. I calmed down! In addition, I continued to look after myself, eating the right kind of food and cooking 'seriously'. Fresh, all fresh ingredients and lovingly prepared on an electric cooking ring in an 'unsightly' kitchen – that too made for a strong body and resilient spirit!

I encouraged myself a lot, was very compassionate, I didn't make great demands, regularly paid myself compliments. I'd started standing in front of the mirror to encounter the soul in my eyes. I'd say: "Sylvia, I love you". I also felt the love I felt for myself. It really did work and I recommend my clients and everyone else to do the same. Stand in front of the mirror and tell yourself you love yourself. Loving someone starts with yourself. Opening up your heart.

Fortunately, I still had some of the money left from my inheritance, around 6,000 euros. Nevertheless, it runs out quickly when you don't have a regular income. I had my strength back and started networking again. Soon there were some new clients for coaching and made-to-measure clothes. I 'received' them all in my anti-squat home and that in itself was an experience for them, having an appointment with me. Six months later and funds were getting lower. I needed more certainty about my earnings. For years Roel's mother had been cared for and cosseted by a private health care agency. I phoned the owner to make an appointment and was taken on as an 'untouchable'. For a certain number of days, a month, one day meaning you were on duty for 24 hours. Back in health care, where I once started as a nurse (Bethel Hospital) and mental health care (PPIA). It took some getting used to: taking care of an old woman in a wheelchair who was accustomed to getting her own way for anything and everything. She was very demanding. She had dismissed a lot of colleagues in the course of two years and several had left of their own accord. From the start, I enveloped her with my love, lovingly cared for her. I started with my hair up, politely knocking on her door or waiting for her bell to summon me. Slowly, I began to introduce my own style and tempted her with my love, to meet up in a dance together. Now I wear my hair long, I often sit with her and she loves being cosseted. My heart and my compassion have grown by taking care of her. When she is resting or watching television, I sit in her office writing. My ex-husband, Roel, thought it was beneath my station to do that kind of work. I don't have criteria with respect to above or below my station. What's important is whether or not it's satisfying. His attitude confirmed our great differences yet again. Our criteria are so different. Mine mean: free to love. It's something you yourself feel inside and others see it in your eyes. They feel it too. Feeling and being free to follow your heart – your heart shows you the way!

I had also enlisted the aid of an agency as I wanted to market myself more as a brand. My brand as Sylvia Duijm. A combination of my work as a coach, healer and 'designer' for a woeful interior and exterior. I didn't manage too well establishing myself as a brand, not 'ripe' enough in terms of ideas and self-confidence. It takes loving attention as well as clear vision and focus. I believe, as no other, that ripening is important and there comes a moment that 'the time is ripe'! Like now: the time is ripe to write a book…

I was still a member of the Industrieele Groote Club (ICG) and I also joined the Maatschappij, an enterprising network since 1777. That was all good for networking and making up for living 'anti-squat'. It added to my style. I continue to think it's important, 'style'! An anti-squat home and sometimes parking my sports car at the dilapidated building. Style is something you have, it's hard to learn.

As a man's woman I got to know more men, it enriched my life as a woman, sexually and also as inspiration for my male side, being someone who takes the initiative, examines new impulses, organises, inspires, my daring and daring side, plus my emotional and spiritual side.

As my friend Debby with a dual handicap would say: "In that way you use more of your brain!" She was intended to model for me in the fashion show that I was planning for the thirteenth International Day of Persons with Disabilities, for my fashion line Deux Pièces by Sylvie D. Sadly, the organiser hadn't got his act together financially and the show couldn't go on. I'd done all the work for nothing. Literally and figuratively. Debby didn't want to lose me, and that was fine with me. We see each other every six to eight weeks and she rings me once a week. I'm an important person in her life because my thinking doesn't run from A to B, and I'm full of surprises. That's not something she's familiar with, also her entire surroundings are structured. She's very scared we'll lose touch. I bought a small art work for her, a little bird. It stands on a shelf above her desk. It symbolises freedom; I fly out and I fly back in, you never know when, but I always return. It gives us both security.

As far as getting to know more men was concerned: they all contributed to my development and I still see them, as friends, with no sex. Once I was living alone again I soon bought all kinds of books to help me examine, to stimulate my own sexuality, and enjoy myself. I discovered that I gave my male partner too much responsibility for my pleasure. You are yourself responsible for a wonderful orgasm, making love is a joint responsibility – here again 'dancing together'. Of course, it's nice if the other person intuits what you feel, what you enjoy, and wants to dote on you. You yourself have the key. Your sexual energy is your primal energy – the most important energy to generate 'flow', making you feel attractive for yourself and so for the other party. I sometimes say jokingly I had a 'biscuit barrel' full of my men when I was living at the anti-squat place, two from the IGC and my 'fabric man', with whom I had kept in touch. The way I put it is somewhat over the top, but actually I leaned heavily on those three men, and they on me – we nourished one another. With one I nourished my spiritual desire, with the second my sexual desire and further growth, and with the third my mental, emotional need. I shared these three perspectives with all three men, but with each the emphasis was different. Of course, I wanted everything combined in one person, but I hadn't found him yet.

After a year of living in the anti-squat place, I looked up Bronja again. She is the psychologist whom I consulted after my youngest daughter had left Roel's house. I wanted to see if, with hindsight, if I had done everything to evaluate my step to leave Roel, and, should I ever take the same step with another man, if it would be the right thing. Talking to her helped me a lot, my own pitfalls became increasingly clear: pleasing, wanting to give and receive boundless love, listening insufficiently to my inner voice in order to recognise the signals, the interference, the aspects that are often apparent early on. Also, understanding the other person well, sensing why someone says or does something is so important, not indiscriminately assuming, often as a kind of security. In that way you hear what you want to hear.

The most important – the absolutely most important – proves yet again that you must love yourself, know what is important for you, what your standards and values are. Only then can you attune yourself, with your heart as the indicator.

As a member of the IGC I was invited to a country house to attend a meeting with a clairvoyant, a man called Carl Spall. Amazing – he singled me out. Told me my decision to leave Roel was the right one, that I hadn't had an easy life and that I myself had played an important role in it. He referred to my two daughters and he described the man I would meet the following year, in September 2012, the man who would become my husband. I forgot all about him!

I was working hard at the time, another fashion show planned, this time in the Handbag Museum. The previous one had been in Krasnapolsky Hotel. Both free of charge for me, all frills included. I was holding more workshops in which I communicated and shared what it was that brought me closer to love for myself (and still does). I gave the workshops in my anti-squat place, with the caretaker's knowledge! I was growing, and the participants thought the world of me. I was their example and their heroine. It was good for me, good for my self-confidence.

Meanwhile my father had had a TIA, the day after my youngest daughter received her bachelor's degree in Sociology. He died two weeks later, without having suffered for too long. On the way home to the anti-squat building after a visit to my father, I was rung and asked if I would return. I picked up my youngest girl, the oldest would go there in her own car. We were one minute too late. My feelings were dualistic, as they had been with my mother's death. Sorrow and relief. In the end I had managed to form a frank, mutual relationship with my father. We told each other what we thought, no holds barred. Unfortunately, my father would frequently tell other people what we'd said, often without the context. It invariably led to misunderstandings. His concerns about my lifestyle, as well as my appearance – I wanted to look feminine –formed a slight impediment. It was always hard for him: he thought I was too sexy! His death liberated me further from what was 'correct', with concomitant inhibitions and fears. I returned to him what was his due, and it liberated me further. Free to love!

His cremation was very confrontational for me, bringing home how lonely I felt in my own family, and my place in it, how separate I felt and how I myself had been the cause. I'm discovering to a growing extent that you create separateness yourself. You have an opinion about something and that produces separateness. The situation does not determine how you feel, how you deal with it does.

My father had been preoccupied with his cremation for years. Everything was ready, a whole 'scenario': what he wanted to be dressed in, where the cremation would take place, where he would 'lie in state', who was allowed to attend and stay for a meal on the day of the cremation, and who would just be given coffee or tea, what music would be played – everything organised in detail. My sister and I knew where the papers were kept, in the drawer of the tea-table, and also his wish (despite my untidiness, I knew where I could always find that paper in my own drawer) that if he had an accident or the like, causing irreparable damage, he didn't want his life to be prolonged.

When he died there were different papers in the drawer – he wanted a private cremation, so my daughters and partners, their father Jeroen, my ex-husband Roel, if he wanted (Roel got on well with my father), my sister and my father's lady friend Truus with her family. The group was too small to my mind. I would have liked my girlfriends whom my father knew to be there. They would be a great comfort to me. His latest 'wish list' did not include them.Moreover, I'd had a fierce clash with Truus about her role at my father's sick bed. If there were a lot of people present – friends, acquaintances and relations – you can conceal some things and it is easier to gloss over the 'painful' family situation. It was awkward: Jeroen, Roel, Truus, her children whom I hardly knew. An alienating farewell.I was there in body, but my mind was elsewhere. After the cremation, we were back outside within an hour. My daughters and their partners went for a walk with Jeroen and Roel. I didn't want to join them. I could feel the tension between Roel and me and I was 'shut off'. My sister had arranged to go for a walk with a friend who was to meet her half an hour later. I asked if I could go with them, because I was moping around and felt lonely. They preferred to go alone. I drove round in my little sports car, crying, desperately lonely. I decided to ring my 'fabric man'. Of course, he had no time then, I'd be welcome at 5 pm. I drove to Muiderberg. Had a towel and a bikini in my car. I got talking to a woman who was also mourning a loss. I hadn't seen the harbour-master – coincidentally also called Jeroen – for a couple of years. He recognised me right away. I'd often been surfing there, and he'd also given me sailing lessons. I had plenty of distraction that afternoon. But the sorrow remained. My fabric man rang. Business was quiet, so he was closing early, I could go around. I hadn't wept so copiously in years, it was wonderful to share my sorrow in that way, everything resurfaces and coincides when someone dies. He was there, for me, completely. His coat was covered in snot and tears. He was a real comforter. When I calmed down he said: "I really want you!" – to which I replied: "Your comfort was wonderful, so loving. I want to leave it at that". He understood, and we parted company, lovingly. Free to love.

Time passed. Time to leave the anti-squat – I had to be out by 1 October 2012, but it was a month later in the end: 1 November. Fortunately, because my fashion show of Deux Pièces by Sylvie D in the Handbag Museum was on 30 September. That would all be a bit too much.

I had met Erik during a network evening. His eyes made an impression on me. I hadn't wanted to go to that evening get-together. I was feeling sad, tired, a bit worn out. It was all overwhelming, what with the fashion show and moving to a new house. But I went, fortunately. I'd taken flyers for the fashion show. Didn't pay any attention to Erik. But his eyes stayed with me. Eyes that had given me such an encouraging and curious look. And I felt I'd looked at him in the same way. I looked him up on LinkedIn and a week later we arranged to meet. He was the man in the prediction Carl Spall made a year before. Erik is the love of my life. I think he's wonderful, on the inside and the outside. If I were a man, I'd like to be like Erik – and the opposite is true. He also thinks I'm wonderful, on the inside and the outside! We can be completely ourselves when we're together. Our communication is open and sincere, however difficult that may be sometimes. Erik, like me, is in a process – one of developing deep love for yourself, enabling you to take the next steps. As he says: "I must first be able to walk properly and then I can go through fire for you. Be patient, have faith!" I do have. I have faith that the universe takes good care of Erik and of me. That if we are destined to be together, it will definitely happen.

I was so happy when I awoke on my birthday, last Monday 13 January 2014. First, I woke at 6 am and thought: "I'll sleep on a while". Then it was eight o'clock. I was the first to wish myself a happy birthday, telling myself: "Congratulations Sylvia. Great that you were born. We're going to celebrate big time!" I was radiant, made breakfast in bed for myself. Took a Tarot card for the coming year – it was the 'Fool Child'. It stands for confidence, spontaneity, openness, playfulness, light and love…

Aren't I the lucky one! It was a fantastic birthday. I made a blueberry pie for the first time. It was delicious, though it looked somewhat less delicious. Too many berries on top, and so top-heavy. It collapsed when I served it. According to Erik it suited me! He arrived at 4 pm to have some pie, just after I'd finished my chapter 'My relationships'. I wanted to finish it at all costs. I wanted to leave the sad times behind.

Hiding behind a huge bunch of red roses, he emerged from the lift. I fell into his arms, as best I could with him holding the roses. Wonderful. The love of my life was there. We put candles on the part of the pie that was still standing, lit them and blew them out in one go…I could make a wish! The wish that Erik and I would share our life together, through thick and thin. He gave me a lovely book with 1001 historic places in the world. I was allowed to choose a place and we would go there on our first trip abroad together. I chose – we're going to Glastonbury Tor in England. It is the location of the planet's heart chakra and I wanted to further join our hearts together there. There's no better place to take a second step. Erik took the first step, coming to my birthday drinks party and meeting my family and partners, my sister and some friends. We both felt so happy and fortunate. A wonderful gift for this 'lucky one'.

Remember, happiness is not automatic, it is a choice and that choice requires upkeep, care. Given care things grow.

And now I'm working hard on my motto:
Free to love!

Afterword

This was nearly headed 'aftercare' – it was automatic! I still work as an 'untouchable' and this is my weekend for caring, alongside my opportunity to do some writing in 'my' lady's study. I've just had brunch with her and I recalled the title of a book by the Dutch writer A. den Doolaard, translating as *Together is Twice Alone*. There's no more contact… her mind is wandering, her body is waiting for death, and I weep inside.

Yet the word 'aftercare' is correct too. In *My Escape to Love*, my life story, I have told candidly about everything and everyone, sparing no-one. I couldn't be merciful. It is my story, with my sadness, my fear, my pain. But also, my story with my joy, my love, my pleasure. You never experience something on your own, someone else is needed and that is who I want to write about now. First of all, my mother: the book starts with her, my passage through her birth canal.

I loved my mother a lot, as a child wanted to feel her love, which proved to be difficult. And I couldn't command it. When a child, my mother had little experience with a loving home and so spent her whole life searching. She did love her daughters a lot. I, the youngest, was very special for her. She used to say: "Sylvia is a special child". Later too, when I was an adult, she thought I was special and was proud and happy about me. Proud because I did what I wanted and took full responsibility for it. Happy because I was her ray of sunshine! She regularly said: "There's my ray of sunshine" and she would beam. We were able to share a lot later in life – about love, life and afterlife. We were also able to wipe clean the slate of our shared past. She gave my children the love she had been unable to give her own children, in abundance.

Thank you, Mum!

My father, an exceptionally erudite man, far ahead of his time. He wanted one thing for his daughters: that we would become independent women, capable of taking care of ourselves, emotionally and financially. He often had his doubts about me: "We must take care of you for when I'm no longer here". Oddly enough: I took/take care of myself! Not in the traditional way, and that caused worries. My father was there at the most important moments, those of sadness and joy alike. Financially too, if I was in dire need he'd fork out, at the last minute. He was there, always. Always looking for love too. His home life was even chillier than my mother's. At my mother's home there were feathers and warmth, at his home there was cold and the cane. He too gave my children the abundant love he had been unable to let me feel.

Thank you, Dad!

My sister – I've given you a hammering too. The absence of a real sister. A dream sister. You were small at the time and did what you could, and you had dreams of your own. Our sister relationship had its ups and downs. Now we've been in the ups for a long time. I'm happy you're my sister and I often think of you as a friend as well. And I've never told you. And it's even better: you have your sister and you choose your friend! I feel you support me, as Sylvia, and you're also a big support for my daughters, your 'surrogate children', as you sometimes call them.

Thank you, Sis!

My elder daughter: I caused you a lot of pain with my divorces, particularly the divorce from your Daddy. You so much wanted Papa and Mama to be together, and not have them in turns. As I write, I realise how much sadness and anxiety the divorce must have caused you as a six-year old, and the consequences. Nor were you happy about my next marriage. I know that life takes its own course and it can't be reversed. I hope you can forgive me and that it will give you all the space you need for your own process together with the love of your life.

Thank you for your trust and thank you for being my daughter. I am proud!

My younger daughter – I caused you pain in a different way, but with the same basic attitude. With you, as with your older sister, I wasn't strong enough to protect you against the things from which I wanted to protect you. I know you learned a lot as a result, and I know that where there's suffering there's growth.

Thank you for your trust and thank you for being my daughter. I am proud!

Jeroen, the father of my children. We were young then, idealists, and both wanted children. We had them and today carry on fulfilling that wish as parents. When you joined us at my birthday party, I enjoyed seeing how happy you were for me that I have found my Erik, and you said proudly: "Willem (our King) and Maxima (our

Queen) are nothing compared with you!" I also enjoy seeing how lovingly you interact with our daughters and their partners. You wanted to leave the party early, but you stayed on. You were so much enjoying being with our daughters and their partners during my birthday dinner party. I'm proud of you as the father of my children, and vice versa – you're proud of me.

As a family we are understanding better and better what Love with a capital 'L' is all about. Last Christmas we had dinner at my home. We still sometimes wept together about the past, the pain we caused each other, our ignorance…The children witnessed our unhappiness. It wasn't a convivial Christmas, but it was a good Christmas, and if that isn't what Christmas means.

And then there's Yoze, my 'adopted' sister in America. At present she is doing well, even better than 'well'! The fact that she loves herself also contributes to that. She listens better to her body and her body to her. The cancer has started to disappear!

All of us 'lucky ones'…

And…

For my beautiful daughters, who were wanted so very much, and for my readers I have succeeded in regaining my love for myself, Sylvia.

With thanks

Firstly, I want to thank someone from my village of Baarn, my literary agent Dr. J.G. P. Best. He introduced me to Aspekt publishers. Jan thinks quite highly of me, writing: "Sylvia was my source of inspiration when I wrote *Troy's Empire*, my last essay, because she, as no other, knows how hard it is to put forward clearly and frankly truths that no-one wants to face, in the interest of generations to come: people like ourselves who still have to find their way in life.

I would also like to thank Erik for reading my manuscript and for encouraging me to write. He has often asked: "Have you finished your chapter yet, when can I read it?" His unconditional support has helped me to write openly and with love, and our mutual openness has only grown as a result. Thank you, dear Erik!

And then there are Antonia, Yoze and my daughter who asked critical questions concerning guarantees for the privacy of everyone in my book. I might be too easy-going in my approach. I'm an easy-going person and tend to forget that others might be keener on their privacy than I am. I'm very grateful to you for that. My sincere thanks!

Also: to everyone who appears in my book, because without them this story would never have been told. Thank you to all the 'cast'!

I'd also like to mention the protagonists when the book was in its infancy. Francine and Riky who were so supportive when I was taking steps to leave Roel, and in the period that followed. And not forgetting the business 'actors' who have become true friends. I owe thanks to Nathalie (designmix.nl). She did a workshop with me and was so enthusiastic, characterising me as a 'master of passion'! She thought it was perfectly normal: "That's the way you are!" she said. And now I believe her.

There's also Ferry (tunico.nl) who built my website for Deux Pièces, amongst other things, sponsored me a lot and is also there at important times in my life. Thank you, Ferry!

My car dealer Pascal (alfaromeoamsterdam.nl), always encouraging, believes in me, looks after my car and, in addition, found me somewhere to live when I left Roel. Thank you, Pascal!

And lastly, there's Pauline (sirion.nl). With Pauline I did a great deal of 'light work', thanks to which I have grown a lot, spiritually. Pauline's meditation helped to boost my self-confidence, the result being that I now love myself much more. Thank you, Pauline!